W9-CBU-228

THE WAY
PEOPLE
LIVE

Life During the
Black Death

Titles in The Way People Live series include:

THE WAY
PEOPLE
LIVE

Life During the
Black Death

by John M. Dunn

Lucent Books, P.O. Box 289011, San Diego, CA 92198-9011

Library of Congress Cataloging-in-Publication Data

Dunn, John M., 1949–
    Life during the black death / by John M. Dunn.
      p. cm. — (The way people live)
    Includes bibliographical references and index.
    Summary: Discusses the conditions and events that led to the
terrible plague that devastated fourteenth-century Europe, as well as its
impact on those who survived.
    ISBN 1-56006-542-7 (lib. : alk. paper)
    1. Black death—History Juvenile literature. [1. Black death.
2. Plague.] I. Title. II. Series.
    RC172 .D86 2000
    614.5'732'009—dc21   99-23791
                                                                          CIP

Printed in the U.S.A.

Contents

Discovering the Humanity in Us All

Books in The Way People Live series focus on groups of people in a wide variety of circumstances, settings, and time periods. Some books focus on different cultural groups, others, on people in a particular historical time period, while others cover people involved in a specific event. Each book emphasizes the daily routines, personal and historical struggles, and achievements of people from all walks of life.

To really understand any culture, it is necessary to strip the mind of the common notions we hold about groups of people. These stereotypes are the archenemies of learning. It does not even matter whether the stereotypes are positive or negative; they are confining and tight. Removing them is a challenge that's not easily met, as anyone who has ever tried it will admit. Ideas that do not fit into the templates we create are unwelcome visitors—ones we would prefer remain quietly in a corner or forgotten room.

The cowboy of the Old West is a good example of such confining roles. The cowboy was courageous, yet soft-spoken. His time (it is always a he, in our template) was spent alternatively saving a rancher's daughter from certain death on a runaway stagecoach, or shooting it out with rustlers. At times, of course, he was likely to get a little crazy in town after a trail drive, but for the most part, he was the epitome of inner strength. It is disconcerting to find out that the cowboy is human, even a bit childish. Can it really be true that cowboys would line up to help the cook on the trail drive grind coffee, just hoping he would give them a little stick of peppermint candy that came with the coffee shipment? The idea of tough cowboys vying with one another to help "Coosie" (as they called their cooks) for a bit of candy seems silly and out of place.

So is the vision of Eskimos playing video games and watching MTV, living in prefab housing in the Arctic. It just does not fit with what "Eskimo" means. We are far more comfortable with snow igloos and whale blubber, harpoons and kayaks.

Although the cultures dealt with in Lucent's The Way People Live series are often historically and socially well known, the emphasis is on the personal aspects of life. Groups of people, while unquestionably affected by their politics and their governmental structures, are more than those institutions. How do people in a particular time and place educate their children? What do they eat? And how do they build their houses? What kinds of work do they do? What kinds of games do they enjoy? The answers to these questions bring these cultures to life. People's lives are revealed in the particulars and only by knowing the particulars can we understand these cultures' will to survive and their moments of weakness and greatness.

This is not to say that understanding politics does not help to understand a culture. There is no question that the Warsaw ghetto, for example, was a culture that was brought about by the politics and social ideas of Adolf

Hitler and the Third Reich. But the Jews who were crowded together in the ghetto cannot be understood by the Reich's politics. Their life was a day-to-day battle for existence, and the creativity and methods they used to prolong their lives is a vital story of human perseverance that would be denied by focusing only on the institutions of Hitler's Germany. Knowing that children as young as five or six outwitted Nazi guards on a daily basis, that Jewish policemen helped the Germans control the ghetto, that children attended secret schools in the ghetto and even earned diplomas—these are the things that reveal the fabric of life, that can inspire, intrigue, and amaze.

Books in The Way People Live series allow both the casual reader and the student to see humans as victims, heroes, and onlookers. And although humans act in ways that can fill us with feelings of sorrow and revulsion, it is important to remember that "hero," "predator," and "victim" are dangerous terms. Heaping undue pity or praise on people reduces them to objects, and strips them of their humanity.

Seeing the Jews of Warsaw only as victims is to deny their humanity. Seeing them only as they appear in surviving photos, staring at the camera with infinite sadness, is limiting, both to them and to those who want to understand them. To an object of pity, the only appropriate response becomes "Those poor creatures!" and that reduces both the quality of their struggle and the depth of their despair. No one is served by such two-dimensional views of people and their cultures.

With this in mind, The Way People Live series strives to flesh out the traditional, two-dimensional views of people in various cultures and historical circumstances. Using a wide variety of primary quotations—the words not only of the politicians and government leaders, but of the real people whose lives are being examined—each book in the series attempts to show an honest and complete picture of a culture removed from our own by time or space.

By examining cultures in this way, the reader will notice not only the glaring differences from his or her own culture, but also will be struck by the similarities. For indeed, people share common needs—warmth, good company, stability, and affirmation from others. Ultimately, seeing how people really live, or have lived, can only enrich our understanding of ourselves.

Century of Death

Death was a habitual visitor to fourteenth-century Europe. Never before had humanity seen such widespread dying. Famines, wars, and a host of deadly diseases all took millions of lives during the 1300s. But the worst single calamity to wrack this troubled century was the Black Death—a plague that killed anywhere from 24–25 million Europeans between 1347 and 1351. As Frederick F. Cartwright and Michael D. Biddis, authors of *Disease and History*, observe, "The Black Death was not just another incident in the long list of epidemics which have smitten the world. It was probably the greatest European catastrophe in history."[1] Anywhere from 25 to 40 percent of the total population of Europe died from this plague. Similar death rates took place in Asia, the Mideast, the Mediterranean, Africa, and as far away as Greenland and Iceland, thus making the Black Death the greatest ecological calamity in human history.

Europeans were horrified and shocked by its lethality. No other disease, nor any war, had ever been so devastating. What must have been most frustrating to those who tried to combat this killer disease was that nobody during the fourteenth century—or for centuries afterwards—understood how this horrific pestilence, or any other disease, was caused or transmitted. This lack of knowledge did not prevent medieval doctors, scientists, and thinkers from offering a profusion of theories about the origins of the Black Death. God's anger, the work of the devil, improper diets, immoral living, polluted air, and supernatural influences caused by stars and planets were just some of the ideas advanced by those desperately trying to explain why this terrible disease ravaged Europe. Nor did it stop those same people from concocting bizarre treatments. Many, for example, believed that victims of the Black Death should have their veins opened up by a surgeon to drain them of corrupted blood. Some doctors applied dried toads to their patients' open sores to soak up evil toxins. A host of preventative measures were also used. To avoid the plague, Europeans ate special diets, breathed pleasant vapors, and wore religious charms. Many also engaged in stranger practices. Some Christians, for example, sought the bones of dead holy men and women to protect themselves. Others whipped their naked backs to appease God and save mankind from the Black Death.

Modern Explanations

Today, the medical community offers a sounder explanation of how the plague was transmitted. Most experts suspect that a tiny flea called *Xenopsylla cheopis* was largely responsible for transmitting the *Yersina pestis* bacterium that causes the disease. In normal times, this flea survives as a parasite that bites and sucks the blood of small mammals, including the black rat, which may have been a primary carrier of the disease in the fourteenth century.

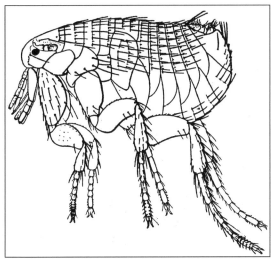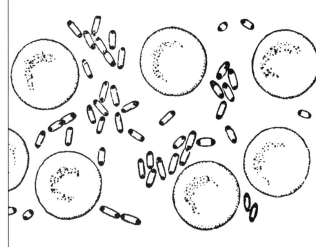

The rat flea (left), or Xenopsylla Cheopis, *carried the bacteria that caused the Black Death. (Right) A magnified view of the plague bacteria.*

How the flea spreads the disease to human beings is a rare and complicated process. First, the deadly bacteria finds a home inside the stomach of the flea. Here it thrives and multiplies rapidly until it becomes such a large mass of cells that it creates a blockage in the flea's digestive system that prevents the insect from swallowing any more of its blood meal. At this point, the flea regurgitates a mass of deadly microbes back into the rat's blood and infects the rodent. A rat can survive with a small amount of the bacteria in its system, but when the bacteria exceed a certain limit, the rat dies an agonizing death. When that happens, the parasitic flea looks for a new host, preferably another rodent. But if rodents have become scarce because of the plague, the flea settles for any other warm-blooded creature, including human beings. Making this journey to human flesh is not hard for the flea to do. Writer Charles L. Mee Jr. observes,

When a rat flea senses the presence of an alternate host, it can jump very quickly and as much as 150 times its length. The average for such jumps is about six inches horizontally and four inches straight up in the air. Once on human skin, the flea will not travel far before it begins to feed.[2]

Normally, the *pestis* bacteria is a problem common to rats and other rodents, not people. But a change in climate during the fourteenth century may have set into motion severe ecological disturbances that caused rats to come into closer contact with humans and thereby have greater opportunities to spread the disease.

Forms of Death

Like many other infectious diseases, the Black Death assumed various forms as it spread through human populations. The most common was the bubonic plague, which was spread to humans by flea or rat bites. Early symptoms for this variant of the disease includes chills, high fever, delirium, vomiting, and rapid heartbeat. Because these characteristics

A plague victim receives treatment. Those struck with the disease often suffered chills, delirium, high fever, and vomiting.

resembled those of other diseases, many people of the fourteenth century often were unsure at first which disease had visited them. All doubt vanished, however, with the appearance of the unmistakable buboes, or inflamed swellings in the victim's groin, armpits, and neck. Enlarged to the size of small eggs, these swellings filled with pus and other septic fluids. Bleeding underneath the skin also caused tiny dark spots to appear on the skin's surface. Victims often went into shock. Many collapsed and slipped into comas. Though not everyone died from the plague, death overcame a majority of sufferers within three to six days as the bacteria swept through their brain, lungs, and kidneys.

Another variant was the pneumonic plague—a respiratory illness that developed during the colder months. An even more lethal variety of the Black Death than the bubonic, the pneumonic plague often killed its victims within a few hours. In addition, the pneumonic variety, unlike the bubonic plague, was spread directly from one human to another by a sneeze, cough, or touch.

The most virulent, yet rarest, strains of the Black Death were the septicemic and enteric. Bacteria cells that cause the septicemic plague invaded and overwhelmed a victim's bloodstream, while the enteric form destroyed the digestive tract. Both plagues killed virtually all of their victims.

A Recurring Plague

Though the Black Death made history in the fourteenth century, it was not the first time the plague had struck humanity—nor was it the last. In fact, the plague appeared again and again for centuries after the Black Death had subsided. Moreover, the disease still occurs today, though most cases are treatable with modern medicines.

Of all the outbreaks, however, the Black Death was by far the worst. It is the most notorious killer disease known to humanity. Though tuberculosis may have killed more people than any other disease throughout history, it did so over a period of many centuries. In contrast, the Black Death destroyed at least a third of the world's population in just a few decades. "It came nearer to the extirpation of mankind than any other evil has ever done,"[3] writes British author and historian, H. G. Wells.

Putting a Name on Death

The killer plague known today as the Black Death or the Black Plague has been called many names throughout history. Fourteenth-century Europeans referred to the disease variously as "the Great Pestilence," "the Plague of Florence," "the Great Plague," "the Great Mortality," or simply "the Death."

Not until the sixteenth century did the plague become known as the Black Death. Some scholars believe the phrase owes the origin of its name to the dark spots that appeared on the bodies of the infected. Other researchers think Scandinavian writers coined the expression *swarta doden* (meaning "Black Death") to signify the extremely terrible or dreadful aspects of this horrible death.

Regardless of its origin, *the Black Death* was an apt term for a disease that wiped out vast numbers of human beings and inflicted widespread despair, grief, and fear.

The plague also wrought vast social, political, economic, religious, demographic, and even physical changes that reshaped Europe forever. As a popular poem once put it, the upheaval caused by the Black Death was "the world turned upside down."[4]

Life in Fourteenth-Century Europe

When the Black Death struck Europe in 1347, it destroyed a way of life that had taken centuries to develop. European society had arisen from a much earlier catastrophe—the fall of the Roman Empire in the fifth century.

At its zenith, Rome provided stability for millions of peoples from Italy to England and from North Africa to the Mideast. Eventually, though, government corruption, massive economic problems, moral decay, and repeated invasions of barbarian armies brought the empire tumbling down. Law and order soon vanished. Literacy and public education declined. Roads and highways fell into disrepair. Business transactions withered, and the use of money faded. Crime shot up. With the breakdown of civilization, people everywhere abandoned the once prosperous Roman cities and fled to the rural countryside. Here, they hoped to evade dangerous outlaws and seek their livelihood from the land.

Europeans eventually forged a new social, political, and economic system that became known as the Middle Ages (A.D. 500–1500) and lasted nearly eight centuries. Unlike the Roman Empire, medieval Europe was not controlled by a single political power. Instead, various warlords—who called themselves kings—ruled over small self-governing dominions. Next in importance in social rank were the king's friends, relatives, and supporters. These individuals received large land parcels from the king; in exchange, they swore allegiance to him and promised to sup-

ply military troops in times of danger. These warriors came from the lowest rank of nobles, known as knights. Mounted on horseback in a suit of protective armor, these defenders wielded swords, spears, and lances against their enemies and lived by a strict code of honor and duty.

All nobles, regardless of their status, belonged to a small privileged class set apart from the bulk of European society—the unprivileged peasants. Some peasants lived as freemen, but the majority were semislaves called serfs who toiled on farms and lived in huts on estates owned by the nobles. All serfs

A serf makes payment to his lord, in return for security and protection.

Two serfs spend their day working in a village shop, preparing and baking bread.

provided rent in the form of money, goods, or labor, but they also had other payments to make. They paid a tax whenever they received an inheritance or had their grains milled. Payments also took place every time a serf married or when a family member died. Serfs even had to pay to hunt or fish on their lords' lands. Every year one-tenth of their crops and livestock went to their lords.

But serfs received something in return for these fees. For one thing, their local noble—known as a "law-ward" or lord—provided law and order for the entire local community. He also kept bridges and roads in repair and protected the serfs when danger came.

The Life of Serfs

Serfs spent most of their days planting, nurturing, and harvesting staple crops such as wheat, barley, and rye. Some, however, worked in village shops and made useful items such as shoes, tools, barrels, soap, furniture, bricks, and cooking utensils needed on the manor.

Despite their hard work, most serfs remained poor their entire lives. Neither they nor their children had many opportunities for social advancement. In some regions, nobles treated them as mere property. Serfs could be sold in France. In England, any serf that ran away from the manor was likely to be tracked down like an escaped prisoner and returned to his lord.

Despite these abuses, most serfs were glad to live and work on a manor. Ever fearful of marauding gangs and armies, they needed the armed protection provided by lords and their knights. They also depended on the manor for work, food, shelter, and fellowship.

A typical peasant home was a simple cottage with a dirt floor and thatched roof of straw. Its walls were made of wood, clay, or mud. Inside the dwelling, an open fireplace provided heat for cooking and keeping warm. Since chimneys were rare, smoke filled most homes. But peasants generally accepted this inconvenience because they believed the smoke drove out evil spirits.

Peasant homes were also sparsely furnished. Furniture consisted of a few simple wooden tables, benches, cupboards, and an oven. Few homes had beds. Instead, most families slept together on thatches of hay or straw. Many serfs also shared their homes with their livestock—cattle, pigs, and chickens—

Peasants participated in festivals on religious holidays or Sundays. The festivals gave them an opportunity to eat, drink, play games, tell stories, and rest from work.

along with pets such as dogs and cats. Not only were these creatures safe from predators and thieves that lurked outside, but they also provided extra body heat for the family when cold winter winds blew through the cracks and crevices of the poorly sealed houses.

Vermin were also always present. Mice and rats—the carriers of the Black Death—found it easy to burrow into the walls of the rough-hewn houses. Thus, they were never far from humans.

Peasant meals were plain. Breakfast consisted of porridge, and lunch was often a serving of whole wheat bread and cheese. For supper, serfs ate pottage, herring, greens, apples, pears, and various vegetables grown on the manor. Meats, such as bacon, beef, and mutton, were only rarely available and were usually rancid. Serfs drank milk, ale, wine, and mead—a type of honeyed beer.

Even this simple diet depended on good harvests, however. All too often, bad weather, mice, and insects damaged and destroyed crops and caused starvation across Europe.

Though Europe's peasants spent most of their waking hours working, they also enjoyed several hours of leisure each week. No work took place on Sundays or during the many religious holidays. On these occasions, young men competed against each other in various ball games, wrestling matches, and weight-throwing contests. Men, women, and children also attended festivals and watched jousting matches between lance-bearing knights on horseback. Many watched organized rooster fights. In the evening men and women gathered in homes or local taverns, where they drank, ate, played cards and games, danced, sang, and told bawdy stories by firelight.

Life of the Nobles

Nobles, meanwhile, enjoyed a somewhat higher standard of living. A typical lord, his wife, and family lived in a large but simple three-story house located not far from the village. The dwelling had several rooms, stone or tiled floors, windows made of oiled paper, and whitewashed walls decorated with tapestries, banners, and weapons. Since the home also served as the place of protection for the entire village in times of danger, many lords erected stone castles for even better security.

Unlike the peasants, who wore simple clothes made of skin, leather, or homespun wool or linen, nobles donned much finer apparel to flaunt their wealth. As author Will Durant describes,

The lord of the manor dressed himself in a tunic, usually of colored silk, adorned with some geometrical or floral design; a cape covering the shoulders, and loose enough to be raised over the head; short drawers and breeches; stockings that reached up the thighs; and long shoes with toes curled up like prows. At his belt swung a scabbard and sword; from his neck usually hung some pendant like a cross. . . .

In her leisure hours [the noble's wife] dressed . . . in flowing fur-hemmed robes of silk, dainty headgear and footwear, and gleaming jewelry.[5]

Meals for families of nobles were usually elaborate affairs. Authors Joseph and Frances Gies describe the preparation for a typical everyday dinner served between 10:00 A.M. and noon:

At mealtime, servants, set up the trestle tables and spread cloths, setting steel knives, silver spoons, dishes for salt, silver cups, and *mazers*—shallow, silver-rimmed wooden bowls. At each place was a trencher or *manchet*, a thick slice of day-old bread serving as a plate for the roast meat. Meals were announced by a horn blown to signal time for washing hands. Servants with ewers, basin, and towels attended the guests.[6]

Nobles with their families and guests enjoyed hearty two- to three-course meals of succulent and exotic meats such as pheasant, boar's head, peacock, venison, and heron,

Balking at Hay Making

Among the many duties serfs were obliged to carry out was to help in making hay. But sometimes there were minor revolts against doing these chores, as Frances and Joseph Gies describe in *Life in a Medieval Village*. According to an entry in the court rolls of Elton, England, for the year 1300, several cotters (field hands) were prosecuted,

"They did not come to load the carts of the lord with hay to be carried from the meadow into the manor as formerly they were wont to do in past times, as is testified by Hugh the claviger. They come and allege that they ought not to perform such a custom save only out of love (amor), at the request of the serjeant or reeve [two official positions on a manor]. And they pray that this be inquired into by the free tenants and others. And the inquest [a special panel of the court] comes and says that the abovesaid cotters ought to make the lord's hay into cocks in the meadows and similarly in the courtyard of the lord abbot, but they are not bound to load the carts in the meadows unless it be out of special love at the request of the lord."

along with various vegetables, fruits, and cheeses. They drank spiced wine and ale. For after-dinner entertainment, nobles played chess, dice, and darts. They sang, laughed, danced, and enjoyed harpers, musicians, storytellers, and jugglers.

Reading was uncommon, however. For one thing, books were expensive because they were handmade and rare. Though most noble women, or ladies, read, many aristocratic males scorned the pastime and derided it as being effeminate.

For the most part, literacy in the early Middle Ages was kept alive by another important pillar of medieval society—the Catholic Church. Across Europe at various monasteries and churches, monks and priests read the Bible and various religious commentaries. Certain members of the clergy—called scribes—also copied famous books by hand. Some wrote chronicles, or local histories of their communities. And when the Black Death came to Europe, these documents provided some of the best accounts of the terrible events that followed.

Keeping literacy alive, however, was only one of the church's main functions. It also played many other roles that greatly affected the lives of fourteenth-century Europeans.

The Importance of Church Authority

After the collapse of the Roman Empire, the Catholic Church grew in importance and power. During the Middle Ages, it provided spiritual guidance to millions of Europeans and also assumed many of the governmental and political functions abandoned by Roman officials. For example, the church ran hospitals and asylums for the sick, the elderly, and the mentally ill.

The church also was a major landowner. By the 1300s, it owned 30 percent of all land in Europe. This meant that many European peasants found themselves in bondage not to the nobility but instead to the Catholic Church. In some cases, however, church leaders were expected to render military service like any other landowner. Few Europeans were surprised that their local priest or bishop was also a sword-wielding warrior.

The church's greatest concern, however, was religion. Catholic dogma was taught everywhere in Europe. Local priests baptized the young, heard confessions, and married young couples. They also spoke words of comfort at funerals and administered last rites—a religious ritual to prepare the dying for the journey to their spiritual afterlife. The church also provided religious training and education for boys wanting to become priests.

The importance of the Catholic Church was emphasized by the largest building in nearly every community: the cathedral.

Nobles often lived a lavish life. Here, nobles and their guests feast on boar's head, cheeses, fruits, wine, and ale.

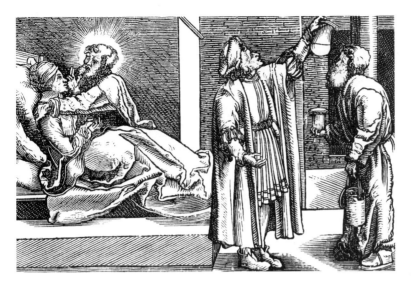

During the Middle Ages, the Catholic Church ran hospitals for the sick. Here church members attend to a patient.

With its huge arches, stained-glass windows, skyward-reaching spires, and massive supporting structures, the cathedral constantly alerted Europeans to the looming presence of the church.

Nearly all Europeans believed fervently in God. And their religious leaders continuously reminded them that spiritual matters were more important than those of everyday life. As historian Robert S. Gottfried writes, "Earthly life was considered ephemeral. What counted was the eternal life of the spirit, God's salvation, and the kingdom of Heaven."[7] Most people accepted church teachings without question. Among them was the concept that the Bible was the literal word of God. No mistakes were to be found in it. To most medieval Christians, heaven and hell were two very real places that awaited departed souls.

Despite their piety, many medieval Christians were generally intolerant of other faiths and quick to persecute religious skeptics, nonbelievers, and followers of other faiths. Sometimes, their intolerance led to violence and death.

Superstition also darkened the minds of most Europeans during the Middle Ages.

Rich and poor alike believed that demons, werewolves, witches, leprechauns, trolls, evil fairies, and banshees roamed the night. Most Europeans, even physicians and popes, were likely to attribute supernatural causes to natural catastrophes such as earthquakes, floods, and epidemics.

Ignorance also marred medieval thinking. Since the collapse of the Roman Empire, much of the classical knowledge of ancient Greece and Rome had been lost or forgotten. As a result, medieval philosophy centered mainly on finding ways to support Christian thought. Medical knowledge existed—but it was mostly wrong. Geography was embryonic at best. No one yet knew how big the earth was or that seven continents existed. The inner workings of the human body were a mystery to even Europe's best thinkers. Scientific knowledge was rudimentary at best. Chemistry, physics, biology, botany, and other fields had scarcely been penetrated. What stars and planets really were and why and how they moved through the heavens remained a mystery. In addition, medieval Europeans understood nothing of the microscopic world of microbes and bacteria that sickened and often killed human beings.

European farmers improved their productivity as a result of agricultural innovations, such as harnesses that enabled horses to plow the fields.

Population Change

For many centuries, Europeans also seemed helpless to keep their populations from declining. During the early centuries of the Middle Ages, Europe's population either dropped or stagnated. But this pattern began to change in the tenth century. Between 950 and 1250, Europe's population shot up from 25 million people to 75 million. This significant increase was the result of innovations in agriculture such as new plows, water mills, and windmills that boosted agricultural output. Farmers also adopted a new type of harness that let them switch from using oxen to more productive horses to plow their fields. And they developed more efficient crop rotation methods that improved farm productivity. In addition, increasing numbers of Europeans converted forests to farmlands which expanded food-growing regions. All of these efforts meant that more of Europeans were better fed and more content than they had been in centuries.

Another result of this dramatic increase in the food supply was that many serfs realized that they were no longer dependent on the manors for their sustenance and ran away. Usually they departed for a town or city where, according to a medieval custom, they could become free persons if they managed to live within a town's walls for a year and a day. And what made this avenue of escape all the more possible was that Europe's towns were increasing in size and importance after having experienced centuries of decline.

What spurred this urban growth? For one thing, Italian seaports, such as Genoa, Venice, and Florence, were growing in size in response to a growing demand for international trade. Their trading ships, powered both by sails and galley crews of oarsmen, regularly sailed to the Mideast to bring back silks, rugs, paper, glassware, spices, sugar, and other luxury goods. A great demand for these Eastern goods came about as a result of the Crusades—a long religious war between European Christians and Muslims fought in the Mideast between 1095 and 1291. Returning Christian warriors introduced these items to Europe along with many new ideas about science, the arts, government, and philosophy, which they had learned from Islamic and Byzantine cultures.

Expanding trade also stimulated the growth of seaports in northern European countries such as Germany and the Netherlands. Annual fairs hosted by city merchants, and even some nobles, also turned small communities into larger, commercially oriented ones. At these colorful and festive exhibitions, such as the great trade fairs that arose in the Champagne region of France, people arrived from many far-flung and exotic places to buy and sell a wide variety of products and to exchange ideas.

Not all of Europe's new urban centers developed for commercial reasons. Some developed near castles for protection. Many church towns, such as Chartres, France, also grew up around famous cathedrals that attracted pilgrims from across the Christian world. Travelers came not only to visit the cathedral but also to see religious relics—items believed to have once belonged to Jesus or a Catholic saint. Many Christians believed that these relics possessed supernatural powers and turned to them for protection when the Black Death or any other devastating calamities arrived.

The Rise of Europe's Middle Class

By the thirteenth century, towns and cities were fast becoming urban centers that wielded great economic and political power. Though nobles ruled some of these urban areas, most were controlled by a new social class of merchants who derived their wealth from money, not land. Beneath them in social importance were artisans such as bakers, butchers, weavers, and blacksmiths. Manual laborers comprised the lowest social class.

Across Europe, many nobles noted the rise of this business class with alarm. Townspeople did not fit into the well-organized feudal society of nobles and serfs. They also had their own ideas about authority, allegiance, and social importance, which they believed had more to do with money than inheritance. In addition, some merchants were as rich and powerful as princes.

In response to these changes, some nobles took action to diminish the rising power and influence of the merchant class. Among

Merchant ships sail toward a European port city.

Before the revival of towns, most medieval Europeans were connected in some way to a manor or rural farming community. This Anglo-Saxon poem, excerpted from Dorothy Miller's *The Middle Ages*, expresses the distress of someone whose lord has died and now has no home.

"Thus homeless and often miserable, far from my kinsmen, I have had to bind my heart in fetters ever since the grave closed over my patron—since I wandered away destitute over the sea amid wintry gloom seeking in my grief the dwelling of some prince, if far or near I could meet with one who would have regard to me in his hall or console me in my friendlessness and treat me kindly. He who experiences it knows what a cruel companion anxiety is to one who has no kind guardians. He is confronted not with gold rings but with homeless wanderings, not with the good things of the earth but with his own chilled breast. He calls to mind the men of the court and the treasure he used to receive, and how in his youth he was continually feasted by his patron. All his happiness has passed away."

other things, they taxed any towns that developed on lands belonging to nobles. They also charged fees, such as tolls on bridges and roads leading to the towns. Sometimes, nobles even resorted to violence and ordered bands of knights to intimidate local town populations and demand payments called tribute.

Town dwellers, however, fought back. They built protective walls around their communities and erected imposing iron-barred gates. Many also took up arms and formed militias. Wealthy cities often hired professional armies for protection. To underscore their growing independence, many town dwellers elected city councils and mayors to govern themselves.

Merchants also had another powerful weapon—money. With it they could buy special favors from nobles and negotiate with kings. Many merchants, for instance, agreed to pay tribute in exchange for charters approved by local nobles that officially recognized their towns as communities of free people.

Town Structure

All towns and cities continued to grow in population until the arrival of the Black Death in 1347. By that time urban populations across Europe ranged anywhere from five thousand to fifty thousand people. Only Paris, Florence, Venice, and Genoa had populations that exceeded one hundred thousand.

When cities became overcrowded, city officials erected an outer stone wall around the existing one to make more room. They then tore down the older wall and used it for building materials within the city. Thus, the cities grew both in population and in physical size.

Inside these stone walls, most working-class people lived in cramped, cabinlike homes crammed next to each other. Every workday, artisans pulled back the ground-level shutters of their homes and opened up their shops and stores to the public.

Affluent merchants and bankers enjoyed a higher standard of living. As a rule, they dwelled in two-story, half-timbered homes with glass windows leaded into place. They dined at carved wooden tables, sat in leather chairs, and stored their belongings in ornate wooden chests.

Not everyone lived inside the town. The abject poor, such as beggars, lepers, and other outcasts, tried to survive in filthy makeshift shacks that ringed the town's outside wall. In addition, the very wealthy often lived outside the town walls in separate walled villas with their own protective garrisons.

Life in a Medieval City

Life in a medieval city was hard for everyone, regardless of social position. Most people toiled up to twelve hours every day, except Sundays and holidays.

But townspeople also enjoyed a level of excitement and energy not found in country villages. Town streets were alive with the sounds of vendors advertising cheese, fruits, meats, bread, silks, jewelry, and items of copper and bronze. Horse-drawn carts rattled down cobblestoned alleys. Street jugglers, singers, astrologers, preachers, magicians, and moneylenders clamored for attention, especially during fairs and holidays. On these special occasions, people ate, drank, danced, and enjoyed a variety of entertainments. Among them were jousting matches that featured armored knights on horseback who competed against each other with long, sharp lances. Sharp-eyed archers also competed for prizes. Also popular with town dwellers was the performance of mystery and morality plays. These plays were based on Christian themes that dealt with the moral decisions facing all humans—decisions that could send their souls to heaven or to hell.

City streets were also used to teach wrongdoers lessons. Though imprisonment, exile, torture, mutilation, and capital punishment were meted out for serious crimes, public humiliation was also used for lesser offenses. For example, unscrupulous merchants, who sold inferior merchandise saw their works burned or destroyed before a jeering crowd. Some offenders found themselves publicly punished in wooden frames through which their heads and hands were locked into place.

The bustle of daily life ceased at dusk when guards closed the city gates. Any late-arriving traveler had no choice but to sleep in one of the many taverns located outside the town wall. Afraid of street crime, most city dwellers locked themselves in their homes at night. Flames of small candles made of tallow or less expensive animal fat illuminated their rooms as they talked, laughed, played cards or musical instruments such as the flute or lute, and prayed to God for protection from the evils of the world.

Medieval city streets were virtually quiet at night, after guards closed the city gates. This protected citizens from street crime and wrongdoers.

Sanitary Problems

Though the cities were the centers of new liberties and economic opportunities, they also presented great hazards. Cities were dangerously overcrowded. Alleys and lanes were often so narrow that buildings on opposite sides nearly touched each other. As a result, fires commonly and easily swept through a town and caused widespread destruction and death.

Towns and cities were also dirty, disease-breeding dumps. Most families lived in cramped quarters that lacked plumbing or running water. Since health or sanitary requirements either did not exist or were seldom enforced, people regularly threw garbage and human waste from their windows onto the mud roads or cobblestoned alleys below. Even the walls of castles were sometimes streaked with human excrement.

Though wealthier families often had latrines and cesspools, these facilities were often shabbily constructed and leaked onto their neighbors' properties. Packs of dogs and pigs rummaged through the putrid-smelling filth that formed a permanent layer of scum along the drainage paths of many cities.

The medieval practice of burying the dead in church graveyards within the city walls also presented severe health problems. In some cases, the decaying matter of corpses leaked from graves and contaminated city wells and fresh water supplies.

Author E. R. Chamberlin provides this description of the streets of a typical fourteenth-century city:

> The streets were a dumping ground for every form of rubbish; only the fact that it was organic and sooner or later became a sludge saved the streets from becoming impassable. In the process of breaking down, it turned into a thick, oily, blue-black liquid which saturated the ground, stained walls all along their base and provided a fruitful breeding for disease.[8]

In such a filthy and contaminated environment, many deadly diseases flourished

---

The Symptoms of Death

In his masterpiece about the Black Death, *The Decameron*, Giovanni Boccaccio gives this firsthand description of what must be the bubonic version of the plague in Florence, Italy.

"The symptoms were not the same as in the East, where a gush of blood from the nose was the plain sign of inevitable death; but it began both in men and women with certain swelling in the groin or under the armpit. They grew to the size of a small apple or an egg, more or less, and were vulgarly called tumours. In a short space of time these tumours spread from the parts named all over the body. Soon after this the symptoms changed and black or purple spots appeared on the arms or thighs or any other part of the body, sometimes a few large ones, sometimes many little ones. These spots were a certain sign of death, just as the original tumour had been and still remained."

and ravaged the populations of medieval towns and cities. Diphtheria, cholera, typhoid, small pox, and influenza killed Europeans everywhere during the Middle Ages. Even before the arrival of the Black Death, three out of four children died before reaching the age of ten.

And amid the sewage, carrion, and garbage, plague-carrying rats abounded. When the Black Death arrived, these vermin served as a ready-made army of silent and stealthy spreaders of death.

Still other problems faced Europe in the early fourteenth century that set the stage for disaster. Among them was the return of widespread famine.

The Coming Plague

Europe's population explosion peaked in the early 1300s. By this time, Europeans had cut down almost all of Europe's forests to make way for new farms. Overused soils on many manors had lost their fertility, and crop yields dropped. Worse yet, the climate changed. All across Europe and in other parts of the world, the weather became colder and wetter. Crops rotted in flooded fields that could not be harvested, and early frosts destroyed blooms on fruit trees and farm crops. Food surpluses vanished, and prices skyrocketed. Famine struck regions of Europe again and again between 1315 and 1317, killing tens of thousands. Twenty percent of the population of Ypres, Flanders (now in western Belgium), starved to death. Similar mortality rates occurred elsewhere in Europe. Even the prosperous port cities were in grave trouble. Giovanni Villani, a chronicler in Florence, Italy, observed that

A merchant uses municipal scales to weigh food for trade. Merchants often learned of the coming plague from traders who had returned from distant lands.

riots by starving people demanding food became so bad in his own city that "it was necessary to protect officials by means of guards fitted out with an axe and block to punish rioters on the spot with the loss of their hands and their feet."[9]

Devastated by these calamities, Europeans also learned in the early 1340s that something even more terrifying was headed their way. Travelers, vagabonds, traders, and sailors who had returned from distant lands told terrifying tales of a coming plague that had already killed untold millions in China, India, and other lands of the East. With growing dread and panic, Europeans wondered if it were only a matter of time before this pestilence struck them, too.

CHAPTER 2

The Spread of the Black Death

Though the origins of the Black Death are unclear, many scholars believe that the first recorded outbreaks of the plague took place in Mongolia in the late 1320s. According to one theory, long periods of intense rain forced rodent populations to flee their native habitats and migrate to new areas. Their movement brought them into more frequent contact with nomadic tribes on horseback who lived on the Steppes, a vast, level, treeless expanse of land in Central Asia. Here, the Great Mortality took its first human victims.

From Mongolia, the disease spread into China and other parts of Asia, turning human existence into a prolonged and unparalleled season of horror and torment. Like so many others around the world, millions of Asians already suffered from a series of natural calamities even before the plague arrived. Droughts and earthquakes between 1330 and 1333 caused widespread famine and death throughout much of the Far East.

On other occasions, however, heavy floods and swarms of crop-destroying locusts disrupted the environment in Asia. Though modern scientists do not fully understand how these ecological changes functioned, many nonetheless believe that these disruptions altered the natural balance between fleas, rats, and the plague bacteria, creating new conditions that boosted the spread of the Black Death.

By 1347 the Black Death had spread across China, India, and other parts of Asia, killing an estimated 25 million people. One chronicler reported that "India was depopulated. Tartary, Mesopotamia, Syria, Armenia, were covered with dead bodies; the Kurds fled in vain to the mountains. In Caramania and Caesarea none were left alive."[10]

Migrating rats and their parasitic fleas spread the infection to yet other lands. But they were not the only carriers. A steady stream of human traffic also helped. By this time a two-centuries-old complex network of roads and sea routes linked Asia, Europe, Africa, and the Mideast to facilitate international trade. The Great Mortality accompanied caravans of cargo-laden camels as they trekked from northern China across Central Asia to the Black Sea. It was also aboard fleets of trading ships that sailed from southern Asia across the Indian Ocean to various ports along the Persian Gulf. Other plague-bearing ships departed southern Asia, rounded the southern tip of the Arabian Peninsula, and finished their journeys at various trading posts along the Red Sea.

The Black Death in Europe

At the western-most terminal ports of these trade routes were several trading colonies set up by Italian merchants who shipped the Asian goods ever farther to Europe. One of these settlements was Kaffa (now Feodosiya), a walled city along the Black Sea built by traders from Genoa, Italy. And it was here at Kaffa that the Black Death was launched into Europe.

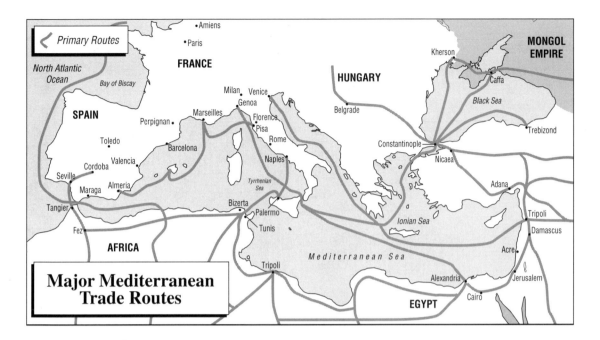

Major Mediterranean Trade Routes

The best-known source of what happened at Kaffa comes from an Italian named Gabriele de Mussis. Though many scholars think de Mussis was not a personal witness to this particular event, most agree that his story offers a plausible, though perhaps exaggerated, version of how the disease traveled. According to de Mussis, hostilities erupted in 1346 between local Turkish Muslims, called Tatars, and Christian traders from Genoa, Italy, in an area north of Constantinople. Fierce fighting eventually forced the Genoans to retreat to Kaffa. The Tatars pursued their enemy, laying siege to the walled city. Trapped for days, the Italians eventually ran low on food, water, and other supplies. Their only chance of survival was to make their way to a nearby fleet of ships and sail away.

At first, this manner of escape seemed impossible. But then something happened that disrupted the siege. "Suddenly the 'death,' as it was called, broke out in the Tartar host, and thousands were daily carried off by the disease,"[11] de Mussis wrote.

The sudden appearance of the Black Death shocked and confused the Tatars. For a while they seemed incapable of acting, but as their death toll mounted, they rallied and took out their grief and rage by catapulting the plague-ridden corpses of their comrades over the town walls to infect the Italians. De Mussis observed:

> The Christian defenders, however, held their ground, and committed as many of these plague-infected bodies as possible to the waters of the sea.

> Soon, as might be supposed, the air became tainted and the wells of water poisoned, and in this way the disease spread so rapidly in the city that few of the inhabitants had strength sufficient to fly from it.[12]

Amid this barrage of diseased, dead bodies, the story goes, the Genoans finally fled for their lives to the fleet of galley ships—large

A priest ministers to victims of the plague.

low ships driven by oars and sails—that waited off shore and escaped. However, the terrified Italians managed to elude only the Tatars. Death also boarded the ships in the form of plague-causing bacteria.

Modern scholars think it is more likely that bacillus-bearing rats infiltrated the Genoan community and spread the pestilence to the Italians before they departed Kaffa. Whatever the cause of the infection, by the time several of the fleeing Italian ships reached their home ports of Genoa and Venice, many crew members were either dead or dying from the plague. When the horrified citizens of Genoa realized what sort of deadly cargo had arrived at their docks, they drove the ships away with flaming arrows. But their actions came too late: The Black Death had already come ashore. As de Mussis observed,

> When the sailors reached these places and mixed with the people there, it was as if they had brought evil spirits with them: every city, every settlement, every place was poisoned by the contagious pesti-

lence, and their inhabitants, both men and women died suddenly.[13]

Twelve other Genoan ships also met hostility when they tried to dock at Messina, a seaport in southern Sicily, in October 1347. Terrified local residents also forced these ships to depart their harbor, but not before infected crew members, or perhaps diseased rats on board, carried the deadly bacillus to the mainland. De Mussis wrote that "the great pestilence came so suddenly that there was no time to organize any measures of protection; from the very beginning the officials were too few, and soon there were none. The population deserted the city in crowds."[14]

Many of the frightened people of Messina fled to the neighboring Sicilian town of Catania, located fifty-five miles away. At first, the inhabitants of Catania welcomed their neighbors. But their hospitality soon vanished when their guests began dying by the dozens from the Black Death. Michael of Piazza, a Franciscan friar, observed that when the Messinians began to die, "[The Catanians] refused even to speak to any from Messina or have anything to do with them, but quickly fled at their approach."[15] Terrified Catanians promptly closed their city to any other outsiders and ordered all healthy people of Messina to bury their dead outside the city gates. Their desperate efforts, however, did nothing to stem the spread of the Black Death across the island country. Soon, Sicilians everywhere died in great numbers as the disease spread.

Civilizations Laid to Waste

Meanwhile, other seafaring traders most likely carried the Black Death to Corsica, Sardinia, Spain, and the eastern Mediterranean. From there, the Great Pestilence made its way to Africa, the Mideast, and Arabia. Within a year, the Black Death overwhelmed the Islamic world, killing at least a third of its population. The famous Islamic historian Ibn Khaldun, whose parents died from the plague, wrote that

civilization both in the East and the West was visited by a destructive plague, which

devastated nations and caused populations to vanish. It swallowed up many of the good things of civilization and wiped them out. . . . Civilization decreased with the decrease of mankind. Cities and buildings were laid waste, roads and way signs were obliterated, settlements and mansions became empty and dynasties and tribes grew weak. The entire inhabited world changed.[16]

Everywhere that the Black Death struck, huge numbers of people died agonizing and horrible deaths. Many victims died abruptly. Some perished within a few hours. Others lingered for a few days after first contracting a burning fever. "Soon the poison mounted to the brain, and the sufferer lost the use of speech, became insensible to what was taking place about him, and appeared sunk in a deep sleep,"[17] writes author Francis Aidan Gasquet.

Next, the disease struck the victim's lungs and caused deep, sharp pains within the chest. The sufferer coughed up blood; his breath stank. Black spots often appeared on

Fear in Messina

In Francis Aidan Gasquet's *The Black Death of 1348 and 1349*, Gabriele de Mussis, an Italian notary who witnessed the Black Death in Italy, offers this description of the arrival of plague-infected ships in Messina, Sicily, in October 1347.

"Seeing what a calamity of sudden death had come to them by the arrival of the Genoese, the people of Messina drove them in all haste from their city and port. But the sickness remained and a terrible mortality ensued. The one thought in the mind of all was how to avoid the infection. The father abandoned the sick son; magistrates and notaries refused to come and make the wills of the dying; even the priests to hear their confessions. . . . Corpses were abandoned in empty houses, and there was none to give them Christian burial. The houses of the dead were left open and unguarded with their jewels, money, and valuables; if anyone wished to enter, there was no one to prevent him."

the victim's body. At this point for most plague victims, death soon followed.

Death tolls mounted as the Black Death raged throughout the Aegean and the Mideast and steadily advanced throughout Italy—the cleanest and most urbanized and sophisticated of all fourteenth-century European countries. Although Italy was highly urbanized and Italians were well educated compared to most of their neighbors, this Mediterranean country was no better prepared for the massive onslaught of the Black Death than any other country.

After making landfall in Venice, Genoa, Pisa, and other seaports in the winter of 1347, the Black Death traveled inland and across the Italian peninsula. Within six months, the disease attacked Italian commu-

nities big and small. Everywhere, people lay racked with fever, disfigured with buboes, and abandoned by those too terrified to even touch them.

High death rates occurred almost everywhere in Italy. In Venice, people died at the astonishing rate of six hundred people a day. Most families in Pisa lost at least two or three members before the plague subsided in September 1348. Siena may have lost at least eighty thousand people. The living horror of the plague also arrived in Parma and Reggio, carrying off as many as forty thousand people.

A contemporary chronicle-writer known as Sercambi recorded how the great number of deaths convinced some Italians that the human race was being annihilated:

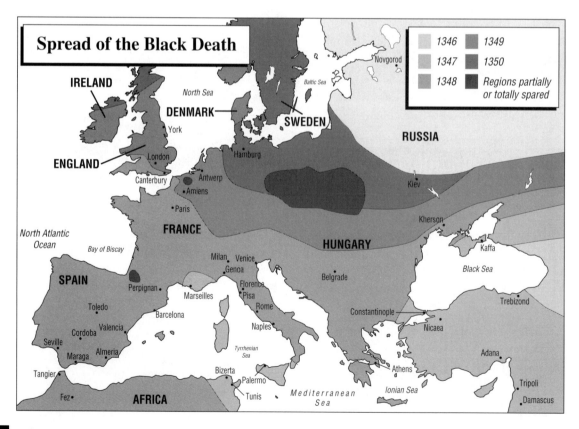

Spread of the Black Death

1346	1349
1347	1350
1348	Regions partially or totally spared

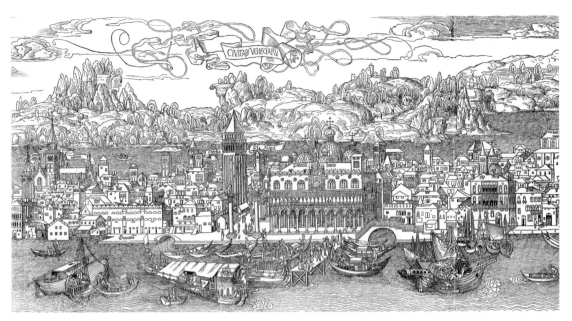

The prosperous city of Florence was among the Italian cities worst struck by the plague.

[In 1348] . . . there began a great dying in Pisa, and from there spread over the whole of Tuscany. And it raged most fearfully at Lucca. During this great epidemic of death more than eighty died of every hundred, and the air was so infected that death overtook men everywhere, wherever they might flee. And when they saw everybody dying they no longer needed death and believed that the end of the world was at hand.[18]

Among the worst hit Italian cities was Florence, a prosperous city on the Arno River. Here, the plague destroyed tens of thousands of lives. The chronicler Giovanni Villani thought that as much as 60 percent of the city's population died. Much of what is known of the disease's deadly conquest of this city comes from the fourteenth-century Italian writer Giovanni Boccaccio. Though the tales in his masterpiece *The Decameron*

are fictional, historians nonetheless consider Boccaccio's descriptions of the Black Death to be an accurate and powerfully moving chronicle of the ravages of the disease. According to Boccaccio,

> The violence of this disease was such that the sick communicated it to the healthy who came near them, just as fire catches anything dry or oily near. And it even went further. To speak to or go near the sick brought infection and a common death to the living; and moreover, to touch the clothes or anything else the sick had touched or worn gave the disease to the person touching.[19]

Crowds of people fled Florence for the countryside. But the rural regions were seldom safer. Many who fled Italy's towns and cities carried the germs of death with them and unintentionally destroyed entire villages. Boccaccio notes that the surrounding country was spared nothing of what befell Florence. The villages on a smaller scale were like the city; in the fields and isolated farms the poor wretched peasants and their families were without doctors and any assistance,

People in villages decimated by the plague often ended up burying their dead in mass graves.

and perished in the highways, in their fields and houses, night and day, more like beasts than men.[20]

And with each outbreak of the Black Death in the countryside, villagers reacted much as their city counterparts did. As the infected sickened and died, survivors ran away and neglected not only their families but also their crops and livestock. As a result, writes Boccaccio, "Cows, asses, sheep, goats, pigs, fowls and even dogs, those faithful companions of man, left the farms and wandered at their will through the fields, where the wheat crops stood abandoned, unreaped and ungarnered."[21] This disruption of food production only compounded the problems besieging Italy.

By the winter of 1348 the worst of the plague was over and Italy was in shambles. Historian Robert S. Gottfried writes, "Taking into account the famines of the early fourteenth century, it's likely that the Italian population was reduced by 50 percent to 60 percent from 1290 to 1360."[22]

But Italy was not a lone sufferer in the community of European nations. Like a vast, rapid, and unstoppable shadow, the Black Death swept beyond Italy to conquer millions more.

The Plague Continues

Not long after the Black Death struck Italy, its presence was detected elsewhere in Europe. Merchants, travelers, pilgrims, and others who fled outbreaks of Italy's Black Death unknowingly scattered the contagion in all directions. Trade ships may have also spread the pestilence to Barcelona, Spain; Marseilles, France; and Tunis, North Africa.

From Marseilles, where approximately fifty-seven thousand died, the plague progressed north and west across France, Europe's most populated country. So many people died at Montpellier, observed Simon de Covino, a Parisian doctor in 1350, "that the number of those swept away was greater than those left alive; cities are now depopulated, thousands of houses are locked up, thousands stand with their doors wide open, their owners, and those who dwelt in having been swept away."[23]

In Narbonne, thirty thousand lost their lives to the plague. But Avignon lost five times as many. A high official in the Catholic Church, identified only as "the Canon of the Low Countries," wrote,

> To put the matter shortly, one-half, or more than a half, of the people at Avignon are already dead. Within the walls of the city there are now more than 7,000 houses shut up; in these no one is living, and all who have inhabited them are departed; the suburbs hardly contain any people at all.[24]

According to another French chronicler,

> When anyone is infected by it dies, all who see him in his sickness or visit him or even carry him to the grave, quickly follow him there. These sick are served by their kinsfolk as dogs would be; food is

A father holds his dead child, a victim of the plague.

put near the bed for them to eat and drink after which all fly.[25]

One of those who personally witnessed the horror in Avignon was Pope Clement VI. In a letter to the General Chapter of the Friars Minor at Verone, the pope wrote of his deep personal sadness caused "by the mortal sickness which is carrying off from us old and young, rich and poor, in one common, sudden and unforseen death."[26]

By the summer of 1348, the pestilence had spread even farther across France. In Paris, the most populous European city, the Black Death killed fifty thousand men, women, and children. During the worst months of November and December, as many as eight hundred people may have died each day.

Before the end of summer, the Black Death moved to the north, where it killed another seventeen thousand people in Amiens. In Normandy, located along France's northern coast, black flags flapped from church towers to announce the local populace's lament of the disease's devastating arrival. Half of all of the residents in the towns of Caen and Rouen in the Normandy region may have died.

"A Staggering Mortality"

Meanwhile, the disease swept to the east and took root in Tournai, where it raged for months. Gilles Li Muisis, the abbot of St. Gile in Tournai, wrote, "Future generations should know that in Tournai there was a staggering mortality at Christmas time, for I have heard from many people who said that they knew for a fact in Tournai more than 25,000 people had died."[27]

By August the Black Death had swept across all of France. An anonymous cleric of Bruges describes the extent of the disease:

In the year of our Lord 1348, that plague, epidemic, and mortality . . . by the will of God has not ceased; but from day to day grows and descends upon other parts. For in Burgundy, Normandy, and elsewhere it has consumed, and is consuming, many thousands of men, animals, and sheep.[28]

Another chronicler of this period, William of Nangis, summed up the widespread impact of the disease on his country: "It lasted in France the greater part of 1348 and 1349, and afterwards there were to be seen many towns, country places, and houses in good cities remaining empty and without inhabitants."[29]

French physician Guy de Chauliac estimated that by the time the Black Death spent itself in France, three-fourths of the nation's population was dead. Many modern historians, however, think this estimate, like many others made in the fourteenth century, may have been exaggerated.

As France suffered, migrating rats, fleas, and infected people continued to spread the Black Death across continental Europe. From France, the plague devastated the Low Countries that make up modern Belgium, Luxembourg, and the Netherlands. "The plague raged in Holland as furiously as has ever been seen. People died walking in the streets,"[30] reported one observer.

An anonymous fourteenth-century writer observed that the disease "raged so terribly in Carinthia, Austria, and Bavaria that many cities were depopulated, and in some towns which it visited many families were destroyed so completely that not a member was found to have survived."[31] In late summer, the Black Death also reached northern Germany and Prussia, Poland, and Hungary.

In Valencia, Spain, three hundred people died daily during the worst of the disease. Outbreaks also occurred in the Balkans along the Adriatic Sea.

For a while the people of Wales, Scotland, Ireland, and the countries of Scandinavia seemed immune to the multiplying horrors of continental Europe during the summer of 1348. Both the English Channel and the North Sea provided a sea barrier to the rapid spread of the disease.

But people in these northern lands knew their luck could not hold forever. They feared that either supernatural means or a contaminated ship or boat would enable the Black Death to make its way to their shores.

For the moment, though, there was a pause in the momentum of the Black Death. But this was a mixed blessing. Unlike the plague's victims in southern Europe, who

Letter to a Friend in the Wake of the Black Death

Quoted in Rosemary Horrox's *The Black Death*, this extract from a letter written to a friend of the Italian poet and diplomat Petrarch expresses the author's painful sorrow and sense of loss in the wake of the Black Death.

"Scarcely a year and half has passed since I returned to Italy and left you weeping on the banks of the Sorgues, so I am not asking you to cast your mind back a long way, but to count up those few days and consider what we were, and what we are. Where are our dear friends now? Where are the beloved faces? Where are the affectionate words, the relaxed and enjoyable conversations? What lightning bolt devoured them? What earthquake toppled them? What tempest drowned them? What abyss swallowed them? There was a crowd of us, now we are almost alone. We should make new friends—but how, when the human race is almost wiped out; and why, when it looks to me as if the end of the world is at hand? Why pretend? We are alone indeed. . . . How transient and arrogant an animal is man? How shallow the foundations on which he rears his towers? You see how our great band of friends has dwindled. Look, even as we speak we too are slipping away, vanishing like shadows. One minute someone hears that another has gone, the next he is following in his footsteps."

were struck down almost without warning, many northern Europeans knew far in advance of the plague's approach and were petrified with worry.

Beyond the English Channel

Many residents of southern England, where the plague was most likely to strike next, knew they should prepare themselves for the worse. But what could they do to fortify themselves again such a disease? Some English religious officials believed the solution lay in having their congregation pray that the pestilence remain on the French side of the channel. Archbishop Zouche of York ordered all parishioners in his district to hold religious processions and litanies twice a week "for the stay of pestilence and infection."[32]

But not everyone, however, took the words of the clergy too seriously. According to author Sir Arthur Bryant,

In days when news travelled only by word of mouth and was carried from village to village along the grass roadways by friars and pedlars, the people of an isolated northern island can have heard little of the fate that had befallen their fellow Christians beyond the Channel. Absorbed in their local affairs, they were more concerned about the weather, the ruin of the crops and the murrain [a disease] that had broken out among the sheep and cattle.[33]

As England anxiously awaited the arrival of the plague, fierce rainstorms pelted the land along with much of the rest of northern Europe. As the Westminster monk and chronicler John of Reading observed, "In 1348 rain poured down in the south and west country from Midsummer to Christmas, scarcely stopping by day or night but still drizzling."[34]

At least one other monk, Henry Knighton of Leicester, believed that the extraordinary rainfall was a punishment from God for the behavior of Englishwomen who attended tournaments, dressed as men, and "wearied their bodies with fooleries and wanton buffoonery."[35] And for this behavior, according to Knighton, God opened the "floodgates of heaven with rain and thunder and lurid lightning and by unwonted blasts of tempestuous winds."[36]

But all too soon an infinitely worse punishment crossed the storm-swept channel and descended on the people of the British Isles with a fury.

Death Bridges the Channel

Neither the English Channel, public acts of piety, nor the vigilance of English port authorities could stop the spread of the Black Death. In August an infected ship from Gascony, France, brought the disease to the English coastal town known today as Weymouth. Another outbreak was reported at the English port town called Melcombe in Dorset. Bristol suffered an outbreak a week later.

Soon the Black Death spread like wildfire across England. The inhabitants of nearby Gloucester tried to keep the disease from their community by breaking off all communication with Bristol, but their efforts were in vain. Soon they, too, were dying from the plague.

Because the south of England possessed many open pastures, fields, and numerous good roads, people were able to flee outbreaks of the disease freely and quickly. But this terrain also enabled plague-bearing black rats, their parasitic fleas, and infected fleeing humans to move swiftly from town to town. As a result, the Black Death shot rapidly through the communities of southern England. This disease also spread rapidly wherever people crowded together

A village crier announces the day's death toll.

in walled towns or cramped Catholic monasteries. An observer at the Malmesbury Abbey in Wilshire observed that

> Travelling all over the south country it [the Black Death] wretchedly killed innumerable people in Dorset, Devon and Somerset. It was, moreover, believed to have been just as cruel among pagans as Christians, where very few were left alive, and then travelled northwards, leaving not a city, a town, a village, or even, except rarely, a house, without killing most or all of the people, there so that over England as a whole a fifth of the men, women and children were carried to burial.[37]

That autumn the Black Death conquered one village or town after another in the south of England as shocked people watched their loved ones burn with fever, vomit, and produce hideous black buboes, mockingly called "God's tokens."[38]

Entire villages were depopulated. As a result, notes Bryant, "The crops rotted in the fields, the church bells were silent, and everywhere corpses were flung, blackened and stinking, into hastily dug pits."[39]

"Dens of Wild Beasts"

People in the north of England heard these astounding reports of wholesale death and suffering and waited in terror for the plague's inevitable arrival in their own region. Bishop Edington, the treasurer of the diocese of Winchester, warned his fellow Christians that a terrible disease had transformed the cities of Europe into "dens of wild beasts" and had "begun to afflict the coasts of the realm of England."[40]

Finally, the Great Mortality moved northward. By November it swarmed into London, which was then England's largest city. Before the plague subsided, 40 to 50 percent of the population of London may have perished. The city would not return to its pre–Black Death population level of sixty thousand inhabitants for another 175 years.

The midlands and northern stretches of England succumbed to the plague by the spring of the next year. Chronicler Thomas Burton, a monk in Yorkshire, remarked on the cumulative impact of the disease on his fellow citizens:

The pestilence held such sway in England at that time that there were hardly enough people left alive to bury the dead, or enough burial grounds to hold them. . . . The pestilence grew so strong that men and women dropped dead while walking in the streets, and in innumerable households and many villages not one person was left alive.[41]

As the Black Death finished off the last of its victims in England, people in Scotland waited their turn. For a while, the vast, thinly populated rolling fields, or moors, checked the spread of the plague into Scotland. This lull may have tempted many in Scotland to believe that they were immune to the pestilence and that its horrors were intended by God to strike down their enemy, the English. Some overly confident Scots were also convinced that the time was ripe for an attack on their vulnerable English neighbors. Henry Knighton, however, reports how the Black Death soon shattered this plan:

The Scots, hearing of the cruel plague of the English, declared that it had befallen them through the revenging hand of God, and they took to swearing "by the foul death of England.". . . And thus the Scots, believing that the English were overwhelmed by the terrible vengeance of God, gathered in the forest of Selkir with the intention of invading the whole realm of England. The fierce mortality came upon them, and the sudden cruelty of a monstrous death winnowed the Scots. Within a short space of time around 5000 died, and the rest, weak and strong alike, decided to retreat to their own country. But the English, following, surprised them and killed many of them.[42]

Making matters worse for Scotland, the retreating Scottish warriors carried the pestilence back to their homes and villages, where it struck down people of all classes.

Next, the plague traveled into the lush, green hills and valleys of Wales and crossed the Irish Sea to Ireland. John Clynn, a

An illuminated manuscript depicts the visitations of the Black Death upon a town.

Franciscan friar of Kilkenny, Ireland, witnessed many deaths in his town and left this poignant farewell in a manuscript he wrote about the unsparing contagion in his part of the Emerald Isle:

> And I, Brother John Clynn . . . seeing these many ills, and that the whole world is encompassed by evil, waiting among the dead for death to come, have committed to writing what I have truly heard and examined; and so that the writing does not perish with the writer . . . I leave parchment for continuing the work, in case anyone should still be alive in the future and any son of Adam can escape this pestilence and continue the work thus begun.[43]

Presumably, Friar Clynn was killed by the Black Death and never finished his work.

By 1350 the plague had crossed the North Sea and swept into Norway, Sweden, and Denmark. Everywhere in Scandinavia people died agonizing, horrible deaths. One chronicler reported that in the Swedish capital the "streets were strewn with corpses."[44] Norwegians told of a ghost ship that drifted off the coast of Norway until it ran aground near Bergen. When local authorities boarded the London wool ship, they found all hands on board dead from the plague. Reports of the Great Plague also came from the far away, thinly populated coastal settlements in Iceland and Greenland.

The Black Death spared very few places in Europe. According to author Francis Aidan Gasquet, "The annals of almost every country prove incontestably that most places were in turn visited [by the plague], and more or less depopulated by the epidemic."[45]

By 1351 the worst of the plague was over. But wherever the Black Death had struck, survivors were filled with terror, disbelief, shock, and dismay. Nothing like this, not even the worst wars in history, had ever caused such massive death. And never before had humans had to deal with death and dying on such a massive scale as did those confronted by the Black Death.

Dealing with the Dead and Dying

Fourteenth-century Europeans were familiar with the grim realities of sudden death long before the arrival of the Great Mortality. People often died frequently and unexpectedly in medieval manors, villages, towns, and cities across Europe. Warfare, marauders, disease, famine, and poor diets regularly took the lives of young and old alike. Few people ever died at an old age.

But even these experiences did not prepare Europeans for the shock and horror of dealing with millions of the sick, dying, and dead struck down by the Black Death. Nobody escaped the havoc wrought by plague; once it struck a human settlement, dealing with death and dying became inescapable features of everyday life.

The Healthy Versus the Sick

Wherever the Black Death appeared, people generally reacted in the same way. Though no one knew how the plague or any disease was really transmitted, they did know from experience that exposure to the sick often invited infection. For that reason, communities invariably split into two factions when the plague arrived: the sick and the uninfected. Most of the latter treated the sick as the enemy to avoid at all costs. According to Giovanni Boccaccio, many people in Florence "adopted the same cruel policy, which was entirely to avoid the sick and everything belonging to them. By so doing, each one thought he

would secure his own safety."[46] People went so far as to abandon their own brothers, sisters, spouses, and even children if it meant a chance for survival.

Similar conduct occurred in other cities besieged by the Black Death. Chronicler Agnolo di Tura observed in Siena, Italy, that "father abandoned child, wife, husband; one brother, another. And no one could be found to bury the dead for money or for friendship."[47]

Healthy Europeans even shunned possessions that had belonged to victims of the Black Death. "The goods and chattels bequeathed by the dead were given wide berth by all, as if they too were infected,"[48] noted one Austrian chronicler.

No matter how wide a berth the living kept between themselves and the sick, the plague spread. When the pestilence first appeared in many places, the first to sicken and die were most often the poor. This led many observers to conclude that the Black Death was mainly an affliction of destitute people and not of the upper classes. Scottish chronicler John of Fordum observed that the Black Death, "attacked especially the meaner sort and common people—seldom the magnates [barons]."[49]

Some people even thought the poor deserved their fate and were intended by nature to serve as society's natural victims during a calamity. Alessandro Righi, a physician in Florence, spoke of the poor as a purifying organ that functioned for the benefit of the rest of the community: "Nor can they transmit [the infection] to others, and therefore it is neces-

A fourteenth-century illustration depicts two plague victims covered with pus-filled buboes.

sary, that if anything evil is in the city, they receive it and hold it as they are the glands of the city."[50]

The connection made between poverty and the Black Death was not entirely false. The poor lived in filthy conditions. Diseases of all types—including the plague—often showed up first in the squalid homes and neighborhoods of the poor.

Unlike the rich, poor people lacked the financial resources to flee the Black Death or to isolate themselves in castles, chateaus, and mansions. Many poor people resented the apparent immunity enjoyed by the rich and concluded that the wealthy classes had caused the disease.

All too soon, however, the Great Mortality proved that the advantages enjoyed by the rich were fleeting. The plague invariably reached them, too. Privileged Europeans soon realized that their money and power had failed to protect them from the disease. This popular fourteenth-century verse reveals the dawning realization that everyone was indeed a potential target of the Black Death:

> Sceptre and crown
> Must tumble down
> And in the dust be equal made
> With the poor crooked scythe and
>   spade.[51]

City Authorities Respond

Local authorities did what they could to protect their communities. But all too often the plague killed many of these officials as well and hampered all governmental responses. Others ran away. In some places, governments were so enfeebled that they ceased functioning until the plague passed. In London, for example, Parliament was suspended by royal decree on January 1, 1349, and again on March 10 as the plague continued to kill.

The few government officials who remained did their best to carry out their official duties. Without question, dealing with the plague was their most pressing responsibility. The first official act for many was to reduce the movement of infected people. Officials in Venice, for instance, set up strict quarantines on ships entering their harbors. No one on board was allowed to enter the city for at least forty days. The penalty for violating this law was death. Though it was hard to enforce, some authorities banned travel altogether. Officials in Pistoia, Italy, proclaimed such an ordinance on May 2, 1348:

> So that the sickness which is now threatening the region around Pistoia shall be prevented from taking hold of the citizens of Pistoia, no citizen or resident of Pistoia, wherever they are from or of what condition, status or standing they may be, shall dare or presume to go to Pisa or Lucca; and no one shall come to Pistoia from those places: penalty 500 pence.[52]

Lives were spared in other Italian towns and cities only because city authorities took harsh, if not cruel, measures to restrict the spread of the disease. In Milan, for instance, officials instructed city work crews to seal up all homes hit by the plague. Everyone trapped inside—both well and sick—were condemned to die. As gruesome as this practice was, it may have helped curb the plague's advance. Milan's death rate from the Black Death was 15 percent—the lowest of all Italian cities.

Isolating the Sick

Isolating the sick became official policy in most towns and cities. Plague victims were sent to special plague hospitals, or buildings and kept apart from the uninfected. Sometimes the plague-stricken were banished. Bernabo Visconti, the lord of Milan, who personally issued many plague regulations for his city, proclaimed that "each person who displays a swelling or tumour shall immediately leave the city." Priests were ordered to examine sick persons and report the illness to "designated searchers under pain of being burnt alive."[53]

Government officials also ordered various cleanup campaigns. Though educated Europeans did not understand the nature of disease-causing germs, most suspected a link between filth and illness. Sometimes, the orders to rid the city of filth came from the highest authority. In 1349 the king of England complained to the mayor of London that "the streets and lanes through which people had to pass were fouled with human faeces, and the air of the city poisoned to the great dangers of men passing, especially in this time of infectious disease."[54] London's cleaning crews, already burdened with disposal of an estimated twenty thousand dead bodies, could do little more than that.

Gruesome reminders of the fate that awaited so many were everywhere—even in the sounding of church bells. In Tournai, France, for example, churches traditionally rang bells to announce funerals. Once the Black Death took hold in Tournai, the bells pealed continuously. According to Gilles Li Muisis,

In all the parishes the priests, the parish clerks and the grave diggers earned their fees by tolling the passing bells by day and night, in the morning and in the evening; and thus everyone in the city, men and women alike began to be afraid; and no one knew what to do.[55]

When the toll reached thirty bodies a day arriving at local parishes for funerals and buri-als, Tournai's city council ordered church officials to cease ringing the bells. In addition, it put an end to all funeral services held in churches. Instead, the dead were sent immediately to the graveyards for swift burial. This action was done to prevent people from congregating and spreading the disease. As another precaution, the city council also forbade groups of mourners to meet at the homes of the dead. Actions such as these may have

Although people did not know the cause of the disease, they did know that victims seemed to be transmitting it. Here, the dead are quickly transported to graveyards.

helped slow the rate of infection, but for the most part, the parade of death continued.

The Everyday Spectacle of Death

Day after day in cities such as Florence, Paris, and Vienna, the living watched from their houses as the corpses of their loved ones and neighbors were carted away like heaps of rubbish. And as more and more people throughout the city swelled up with buboes, vomited, and died, those not yet infected went into a state of terror and shock. Some were so dumbfounded with horror that they appeared drained of all human emotion. "People cared no more for dead men than we care for dead goats,"[56] observes Boccaccio of the plague in Florence.

As death became an everyday occurence in Europe, it was not uncommon for people to witness the death of family and friends.

Daily life became a waking nightmare for both rich and poor. People perished at home, at church, in the markets, and in the fields. Many of the poor and middle classes, says Boccaccio, "ended their lives in the streets both at night and during the day; and many others who died in their houses were only known to be dead because the neighbors smelled their decaying bodies."[57]

The stench of death fouled the air. Sniffing rats caught the odor and moved into the areas to feast on the dead. Vultures, too, darkened the sky above many locations in Europe as they searched for carrion. In some regions, decaying bodies also lured into villages, towns, and cities the most feared of all creatures in the fourteenth century—packs of wolves. In some towns wolves and wild animals prowled city streets and devoured the dead and even some of the living. According to one eyewitness to the Black Death in Italy,

> Savage wolves roamed about in packs at night and howled around the walls of the towns. In the villages they did not slake their thrist for human blood by luring in secret places, as was otherwise their wont, but boldly entered the open houses and tore the little ones from their mothers' sides; indeed they did not only attack children, but even armed men and overcame them. To the contemporaries they seemed no longer wild animals but demons.[58]

Ghastly scenes such as this could be seen all across Europe. As thousands of decaying human corpses piled up, the living struggled with a new problem: what to do with the dead.

The common means of disposing of corpses in fourteenth-century Europe was burial. Christians, who comprised most of Europe's population, expected to receive Christian funerals when they died and to be buried in consecrated ground—that is, a hallowed spot of earth specially blessed by a religious official.

Lack of Burial Space

Guided by church teaching, they believed that on some distant Judgment Day all dead Christians would come back to life. Thus, in preparation for that sacred event it was important to be buried in consecrated land, which was usually located inside city gates. At first, church officials insisted on consecrated graves for the dead. Worries about the spread of infection led many townspeople to demand that plague victims be buried well outside the city gates.

The vast numbers of dead and dying made traditional Christian burial nearly impossible. To address the shortage of proper burial ground in France, the pope consecrated the Rhone River at Avignon so that it could be used for Christian burials. Elsewhere, church officials sought other solutions. Lack of burial space in Florence, for example, forced a halt to the old custom of burying the dead in family graves. The alternative in Florence and elsewhere was mass burial. Boccaccio relates that,

> although the cemeteries were full, . . . [grave diggers] were forced to dig huge trenches, where they buried the bodies by hundreds. Here they stowed them away like bales in the hold of a ship and covered them with a little earth, until the whole trench was full.[59]

The grieving had little choice in the matter; they were forced to accept any grave that was provided for family members and friends.

The urgent need to dispose of the dead took priority over all else. As Gabriele de Mussis, a resident of Piacenza at the time, observed,

The dead were without number, and those who still lived gave themselves up as lost, and prepared for the tomb. The cemeteries failing, it was necessary to dig trenches to receive the bodies of the dead. It frequently happened that a husband and wife, a father and son, a mother and daughter—nay, whole families—were cast together in the same pit.[60]

Conditions were much the same throughout Europe. Many Parisian hotels, which served as hospitals, could scarcely keep up with the steady parade of corpses. According to Jean de Venette, a Catholic friar in Paris, "So high was the mortality at the Hotel-Dieu in Paris that for a long time, more than five hundred dead were carried daily with great devotion in carts to the cemetery of the Holy Innocents in Paris for burial."[61]

Some communities ran out of burial space of any sort, leading authorities in a desperate search for alternatives. In Venice, for example, authorities sent special barges along the city's canals to collect the corpses and transport them to a nearby island for burial.

Proper Christian funeral services became a luxury of the past. Many were buried in a sad and unceremonious manner, as described by Francis Aidan Gasquet: "No prayer was said, nor solemn office sung, no bell tolled for the funeral of even the noblest citizen; but by day and night corpses were borned to the common plague-pit without rite or ceremony."[62]

With priests and grave diggers among the many dead, the job of burial often fell to family and friends. In London, a chronicler observed that

the cemeteries were not big enough and fields had to be set aside for the burying of the dead. . . . Men and women bore their own offspring on their shoulders to the church and cast them into the common pit, from which there proceeded so great a stench that hardly anyone dared to cross.[63]

One grief-stricken chronicler in Siena, Italy, reported what happened to neighbors and his own children:

And in many places in Siena great pits were dug and piled deep with the multitude of dead. And they died by the hundreds both day and night, and all were thrown in those ditches and covered over with earth. And as soon as those ditches were filled more were dug.

And I, Agnolo di Tura, called the Fat, buried my five children with my own hands. And there were also those who were so sparsely covered with earth that the dogs dragged them forth and devoured many bodies throughout the city.

There was no one who wept for death, for all awaited death.[64]

When family members were so sick or shocked and frightened by what was happening that they refused to dress the dead for burial or take them to nearby graveyards, few others were willing to take on such a grim job. One charitable group, the Compagnia della Misericordia, founded in 1244 to assist the sick, made disposal of the dead part of its work. Every morning members of the group walked the streets of Florence dressed in red robes with hoods that covered their eyes, grimly tending to the dead.

But such helping hands were rare. More often the ghastly business of disposing of the dead fell to the city's poorest residents. In Florence, for example, every morning the bodies of those who died during the night appeared on house doorsteps. Hired porters, usually Florence's poorest and most wretched citizens, arrived and carried the corpses away on wooden biers—sometimes three or four family members at a time—to a nearby church or a freshly dug pit for hasty funeral and burial.

With so much attention focused on the dead and dying, other matters suffered from neglect. Law and order, for example, essentially ceased to exist.

Workers remove dead bodies from a hospital for plague victims.

This account by Jean de Venette, a Carmelite friar from Paris, gives his impressions of a strange occurrence that he believed may have heralded the coming of the plague. This text appears in *Readings in World History*.

"In the month of August, 1348, after Vespers when the sun was beginning to set, a big and very bright star appeared above Paris, toward the west. It did not seem, as stars usually do, to be very high above our hemisphere but rather near. As the sun set and night came on, this star did not seem to me or to many friars who were watching it to move from one place. At length, when night had come, this big star, to the amazement of all of us who were watching, broke into many different rays and, as it shed these rays over Paris toward the east, totally disappeared and was completely annihilated. Whether it was a comet or not, . . . I leave to the decision of astronomers. It is, however, possible that it was a presage [omen] of the amazing pestilence to come, which, in fact, followed very shortly in Paris and throughout France and elsewhere."

Taking Advantage

Criminals and social deviants took advantage of the breakdown in law and order to commit acts of outrage against their fellow citizens. Among the worst was a savage group of grave diggers known in Italy, France, and elsewhere as the Becchini and the Monatti. For the most part, the Becchini were convicted criminals who were condemned to spend years, if not a lifetime, manning the oars of galley ships. In normal times, most people scorned and avoided these prisoners. But when city streets became strewn with great numbers of decaying bodies, government officials recruited the Becchini to dig graves. At first, many of the galley prisoners were satisfied to be free of their chains and willingly carried out their newly assigned tasks. The risk of infection paled in comparison to the dismal life of a prisoner.

But as the Black Death disrupted the normal patterns of life, many of the Becchini realized the full extent of their newfound freedom. They moved in gangs through cities and towns, looking for victims. Sometimes, they burst into homes of affluent citizens and demanded money or the submission of the women. Otherwise, they threatened to expose the terrified inhabitants to plague infection. The Becchini robbed, raped, assaulted, tortured, and murdered terrified town dwellers without fear of arrest. "They penetrate into the houses, rob and plunder to their hearts' content, and frequently cut the throats of the sick,"[65] French surgeon Ambroise Paré said of a similar gang operating in Paris.

Some Parisians found it advantageous to falsely accuse their enemies of having the plague. Often, they paid gangs similar to the Becchini to drag the unfortunate victims to plague hospitals where they were locked up and invariably contracted the disease and died.

Ruffians committed crimes elsewhere in Europe, including a notorious band in Russia called the Mortus. According to author Johannes Nohl, the crimes committed by the Mortus were "more dreadful than plague and death."[66]

Escaping the Horror of Death

The plague brought out many different sides of humanity. In contrast to those who preyed on their fellow humans, others responded to the spectacle of death by withdrawing from society. Boccaccio noticed that some residents of Florence believed their salvation lay in forming small private groups and isolating themselves from the sick and from public life in general. The author notes that

> they shut themselves up in houses where there were no sick, eating the finest food

and drinking the best wine very temperately, avoiding all excess, allowing no news or discussion of death and sickness, and passing the time in music and such-like pleasures.[67]

Boccaccio also observed that some of the living had the opposite reaction, spent their time drinking alcohol and living in a morally loose manner. According to Boccaccio, these individuals

> thought the sure cure for the plague was to drink and be merry, to go about

Criminals took advantage of the fact that law and order ceased to exist during the Black Death and pillaged, raped, and murdered without fear of arrest.

Ring around the Rosy
Pockets full of Posey.
Ashes
Ashes
All Fall Down!

Charles L. Mee Jr., writing in *Smithsonian* magazine, gives this explanation for the origin of the well-known child's verse about the Black Death.

"It was from a time of plague, some scholars speculate, that the nursery rhyme 'Ring Around the Rosy' derives: the rose-colored 'ring' being an early sign that a blotch was about to appear on the skin; 'a pocket full of posies' being a device to ward off stench and (it was hoped) the attendant infection; 'ashes, ashes' being a reference to 'ashes to ashes, dust to dust' [in the Bible] or perhaps to the sneezing, 'a-choo, a-choo' that afflicted those in whom the infection had invaded the lungs—ending, inevitably, in 'all fall down.'"

singing and amusing themselves, satisfying every appetite they could, laughing and jesting at what happened. They put their words into practice, spent day and night going from tavern to tavern, drinking immoderately, or went into other people's houses, doing only those things which pleased them.[68]

Such behavior also occurred elsewhere in Europe. According to Nohl, for example:

In Rome, during the plague, brilliant festivals and drunken revels were held. Everyone kept open house not only for his friends, but particularly for strangers. In the same way in Paris, balls, banquets, sports, and tournaments formed a continuous sequence.[69]

Even after the disease had subsided, some Europeans continued to live wantonly and wildly, as if they were unable or unwilling to shed their adopted lifestyle. A fourteenth-century observer in Austria noted that

survivors of the plague, apparently putting the terrible experience right out of their minds, embroiled themselves in many disputes and quarrels over the wealth of the dead, or shamelessly went beyond the bounds of decency and, in many cases, lived with no reference to the law.[70]

Those Who Stayed

Not everyone surrendered his or her moral responsibilities to others. During the plague, many people bravely carried on their daily lives as best they could. They cared for the sick and dying, no matter how great the danger. Love, loyalty, and a sense of duty compelled them to help their fellow humans. Numerous priests and doctors fled, but others also stayed often at their own peril.

Despite their acts of altruism, these humanitarians were as shocked and horrified as all other Europeans. Like everyone else, they, too, demanded to know why this unfathomable tragedy had struck them.

4 Looking for Answers

The presence of the Black Death traumatized Europeans on a scale greater than any previous calamity. "The mental shock sustained by all nations during the prevalence of the Black Plague is without parallel and beyond description,"[71] writes nineteenth-century German medical historian J. F. Hecker. Some modern historians believe that not until World War I (1914–1917) did Europeans again experience shock and trauma comparable in magnitude to what the Black Death inflicted on humanity.

Stunned Europeans also saw their society come to a standstill. Terrorized men and women ignored their daily duties and thought only of survival. Trade dropped off everywhere. Cathedral construction and other building projects slammed to a halt. Taxes and debts were not paid. Merchants and artisans closed their shops. Serfs abandoned their flocks and fields. Physicians, priests, law enforcement officers, and many other government officials fled Europe's population centers and abandoned their official responsibilities.

The Great Mortality also unleased a flood of human emotions. Fear ran rampant everywhere. Some people were so despondent that they gave up all hope and refused to care what happened to themselves. "And those that survived were like persons distraught and almost without feeling,"[72] observed Agnolo di Tura, the chronicler of Siena, Italy.

Across Europe, the living grieved the loss of friends and loved ones. Though some re-

joiced that they had survived the plague, others felt burdened with guilt because they had not died along with their family members. Suspicion also ran rampant as people questioned the horror around them. They demanded to know who was responsible for this disease. Some suspected traitors in their midst. Others blamed evil powers and supernatural forces. Religious figures faulted sinful Christians and others who had offended God.

Though Europeans conceived different causes for the Black Death, they all had one thing in common: a need to know why this terrible thing had happened. Many European thinkers struggled to come up with explanations—and all of them were wrong.

God's Punishment

To many Europeans, the Black Death signaled the end of the world. Priests and lay people alike believed the madness and horror that whirled about them was the fulfillment of biblical prophecy of the final days of humanity on earth. As author Johannes Nohl notes, "The plague was the apocalyptic rider on the pale horse, and all signs which were said to precede the last day were recognized which had been prophesied by Christ, the prophets and the apostles."[73]

Some Christians thought God had abandoned or punished humanity. Gabriele de Mussis expressed the anguish of millions of his fellow human beings:

Death is depicted as a mounted hunter and reaper in this fifteenth-century illustration.

I am overwhelmed, I can't go on! Everywhere one turns there is death and bitterness to be described. The hand of the Almighty strikes repeatedly, to greater and greater effect. The terrible judgement gains in power as time goes by.

What shall we do? Kind Jesus, receive the souls of the dead, avert your gaze from our sins and blot out all our iniquities.

We know that whatever we suffer is the just reward of our sins. Now therefore, when the Lord is enraged, embrace acts of penance, so that you do not stray from the right path and perish.[74]

Across Europe, Christians begged God, Jesus, and the Virgin Mary to deliver them from impending death. Many believed that they had to appease God by performing acts of public piety and penance. Others bequeathed their savings and fortunes to the Catholic Church to gain the good graces of supernatural forces. In 1347 panic-stricken citizens in Lübeck, Germany, stormed their local church to donate their money. The priests, however, feared infection from the crowd and closed the church gates to keep them out. Undaunted, the terrified congregation threw money over the gates and begged for the church's blessing.

The idea that God might bear responsibility for such mayhem sank many Europeans into despair. With the power of the creator against them, they wondered what they could possibly do to protect themselves.

The Ideas of Wise Men

In desperation, many turned to their wise men for answers. In the Middle Ages, thinkers sought guidance from the past. Some agreed with the ideas of both Hippocrates, an ancient Greek thinker, and the Muslim physician Avicenna, who had taught that "comets, auroras, and particularly eclipses of the sun and moon, were the causes and precursor of future pestilences."[75]

In addition, many medieval scholars and doctors accepted the ancient theory that plagues were caused by foul air, for this seemed the only explanation for the disease's rapid spread. These theorists blamed fogs, mists, smoke, and corrupted atmosphere as the primary agents of the disease. Hot and humid winds that blew from the south were especially suspect. Avicenna had speculated that all epidemic diseases started around the equator and were carried by winds to other lands. Objects exposed to bad air were also considered dangerous. "Sea fish are now not generally eaten, men holding that they have been infected by the air,"[76] observed one fourteenth-century chronicler.

Earthquakes were also blamed because they were believed to release dangerous toxic vapors from the earth. In Wales, people spoke of the plague as "death coming into our midst like black smoke . . . a rootless phantom which has no mercy."[77]

Europeans also blamed miasma, nearness to swamps, human excrement, and the rotting of decaying human corpses on battlefields for polluting the air and causing the disease's existence. In addition, they believed that unhealthy living made people vulnerable to the Black Death. Overeating of fruits, too much drinking, and lack of sunshine were all suspected of playing a role in spreading the contagion.

Any noticeable climatic change also fell under suspicion. One theory held that a change in ocean currents killed massive amounts of fish and produced a widespread stench of decaying marine life, which, in turn, created the plague. According to historian Robert S. Gottfried, many scholars also "predicted plague by the colors of the evening sky, heavy rains, persistent mists, violent winds, cloud formations, and less probable phenomena such as raining multitudes of reptiles, frogs, and toads."[78]

Finding the Cause in the Stars

Astrology provided other clues to the origin of the plague. This ancient belief system held that astronomical occurrences of planets, stars, and other heavenly bodies influenced events on earth. Today, most scientists do not view astrology as a science. But such skepticism was rare in the fourteenth century. Most medieval Europeans, even popes and scholars, put at least some faith in the capacity of the stars and planets to sway the destinies of humans. One Italian physician even pinpointed the planets as the cause of "poisonous material which is generated about the heart and the lungs."[79]

Some observers also believed that astrological influences mingled with other supernatural phenomena to cause plagues. An entry in the chronicle from the monastery of Neuberg in southern Austria offered this explanation:

> First, through the malignant influence of the planets and the corruption of the air, men and animals in those countries were struck motionless while going about their business, as if turned to stone. Then, in the countries where ginger comes from, a deadly rain fell, mixed with serpents and all sorts of pestilential worms, and instantly killed everyone it touched. Not far from that country dreadful fire descended from heaven and consumed everything in its path. . . . The smoke which arose was so contagious that . . . those who escaped carried the pestilence with them . . . [to other countries.][80]

When asked by Pope Clement II to explain the origins of the Black Death, an esteemed panel of doctors in Paris concluded that an unusual conjunction of Saturn, Jupiter, and Mars in the House of Aquarius on March 20, 1345, caused the disease. Why this happened was "hidden from even the most highly trained intellects,"[81] according to the panel.

The Supernatural

Because Europeans failed to understand that victims of the pneumonic plague infected others by sneezing or coughing minute particles of mucus onto them, they advanced other explanations. They concluded that a stare from a sick individual passed on the disease.

Physicians suggested that corrupted air passed from one person to another merely by inhaling and exhaling in another's company.

Superstition also ran rampant in this unenlightened age. To many educated and unschooled alike, the world was filled with numerous demons, monsters, and crazed humans who possessed strange, supernatural

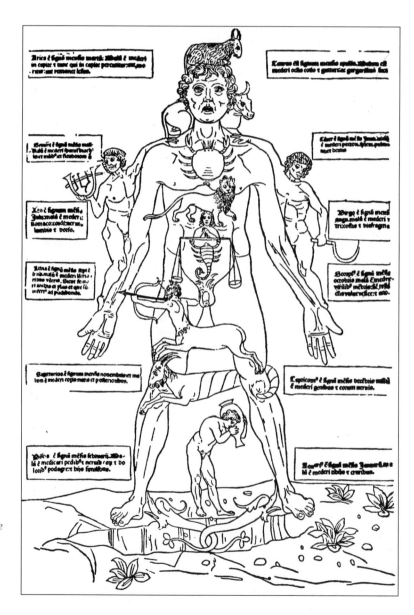

A medieval illustration shows the astrological signs that correspond to different parts of the body. Belief in astrology was common at the time, and some observers were convinced that astrological influences caused the plague.

powers that could cause harm to others. The horror of the Black Death only intensified these fearful imaginings. During the frenzy of the plague, many Germans and Scandinavians swore that they saw the phantom known as the Plague Maiden sail through the nighttime sky and enter the opened windows of one house after another, spreading the pestilence. As Nohl writes, the Plague Maiden needed "only to raise her hand to scatter the plague poison. The spirit was seen in the shape of a blue flame flying through the air and developing on the lips of the dying and the dead."[82]

Elsewhere in Europe, eyewitnesses credited the plague to another specter—the Angel of Death. Nohl notes, "Popular imagination depicted it as a man mounted on a black horse, or else as a black giant striding along, his head reaching above the roofs of the houses."[83]

Many people insisted that the Black Death was the evil work of Satan. Rumors also appeared everywhere claiming that the disease was the work of the Antichrist—a wicked figure that many Christians expected to arrive before the end of time. Many of these tales held that the Antichrist had prepared and spread plague poisons made of aconite, arsenic, napellum, and other foul ingredients. Brother William Blofield, a Carmelite friar at Cambridge, England, reported one of these rumors in a letter to a colleague: "They say that this very year, 1349, Antichrist is aged ten, and is a most beautiful child, so well educated in all branches of knowledge that no one now living can equal him."[84]

An Angry God

More often, however, the deadly plague was attributed to God. Many Christians saw the Black Death as a divine punishment sent to chastise the wicked people of the earth. King Magnus II of Sweden spoke for many when he told his subjects, "God for the sins of men has struck the world with this great punishment of sudden death."[85] The Byzantine emperor John Cantacuzenus described the Black Death as God's retribution for some Christians who supported a Muslim attack on a Christian town in Asia Minor.

Rumors also spread across Europe claiming that God had sent letters to church officials explaining that He was using the plague to punish humanity for a variety of sins. Medieval writers speculated that the sins of excessive greed, sacrilegious speech, usury, adultery, dishonesty, materialism, and worldly pleasure had angered God. A Catholic monk in Westminster, England, even suggested indecent clothing as a cause:

The English . . . have abandoned the old decent style of long, full garments for clothes which are short, tight, impractical, slashed, every part laced, strapped or unbuttoned up, with the sleeves of the gowns and the tippet of the hoods hanging down to absurd lengths, so that . . . [they look] more like torturers, or even demons, than men.[86]

In the absence of a clear explanation for the plague that raged around them, many Christians assigned blame to anyone who was different from the mainstream population. Europe's outcasts—lepers, cripples, Gypsies, and above all the Jews—bore the brunt of public animosity.

For centuries Christian mobs and various government troops vilified, persecuted, and murdered European Jews. Because of their distinctive dress, Hebrew language, Semitic features, and religious beliefs and practices, Jews were easy targets for those needing scapegoats.

As a result of anti-Semitism, Jews were often blamed for the plague and were vilified, persecuted, and even burned alive.

But there were also other reasons for the prejudice against Jews. For one thing, Christianity forbid the charging of interest—a standard banking business practice—considering it a sin. Judaism, however, did not. As a result, Jews became the chief moneylenders in Germany, France, and Spain. This brought them a measure of strength over their neighbors. However, this power also caused resentment and jealousy from Christians who could not participate in this lucrative enterprise.

During the Middle Ages, many Christian zealots also labeled Jews as Christ killers and disciples of the Antichrist. They also falsely accused Jews of committing unspeakable acts. On different occasions, Christian mobs became incensed by a rumor that Jews murdered Christian children and used their blood in their cooking. Another held that Jews defiled consecrated bread used by Christians for communion—a ceremony in which participants drink wine and eat bread in remembrance of Jesus Christ. Though the rumors had no basis in fact, they fueled Christian fears and helped spark outbreaks of segrega-

tion, condemnation, persecution, and mass murder of Jews.

With such a deeply rooted tradition of persecution already in place, the haters of Jews quickly blamed them for the Black Death and fell on them with murderous vengeance.

Blaming the Jews for the Black Death

Once again a false rumor triggered the first attacks. For religious reasons having to do with hygiene, many European Jews obtained drinking water supplies from wells located outside city limits. But this practice made them suspect in the eyes of many Christians. Accusations rang out first in Spain and then later in France, Germany, and elsewhere that Jews avoided city wells because they had poisoned them with a deadly poison made from "spiders, owls, and other poisonous animals."[87] This poison, it was thought, had caused the plague.

Hysteria grew after city officials used torture to force a false confession from a Jew in 1348. As Israeli author and statesman Abba Eban explains,

> The coerced confession of a Jew of Chillon [Switzerland], a poor soul named Balavingus, disclosed the secret formula: frogs, spiders, lizards, human flesh, and —leaving no libel unmentioned—consecrated hosts and the hearts of Christians, all boiled down and ground into a lethal powder.[88]

Soon came other allegations. German anti-Semites charged that Jews poisoned the Danube and Rhine Rivers to destroy Christians. Jews were even accused of poisoning the air to cause the Black Death.

After Balavingus's forced confession, violence against all Jews broke out in Chillon. Soon the violence spread to other cities. At Basel and Freiburg, thousands more were burned in large wooden buildings. In Strasbourg, France, angry mobs hanged two thousand Jewish men, women, and children on a scaffold erected in a Jewish graveyard. Mobs also burned Jews alive in the town square of Nuremberg, Germany. Savage killings also took place in the German cities of Mainz, Erfurt, and Frankfurt am Main. At the city of Worms, Jewish leaders agreed that they would rather die by their own hands than submit to their tormentors. Accordingly, the entire Jewish community set their own dwellings on fire and burned themselves alive. Other Jewish congregations in Esslingen immolated themselves in their synagogues.

Massacres of Jews also occurred in central Europe, where mobs sacked Jewish synagogues and homes and executed them in public places. Similar killings also occurred in Spain and Italy. In France, observed chronicler Louis Heyligen,

> Some wretched men were found in possession of certain powers and (whether justly or unjustly, God knows) were accused of poisoning the wells—with the result that anxious men now refuse to drink water from wells. Many were burnt daily, for it was ordered that they should be punished thus.[89]

Not all of the violence against the Jews can be attributed to hysteria associated with

The Official Use of Torture

The following text, excerpted from Rosemary Horrox's *The Black Death*, was written by city officials in Lausanne, Switzerland, on November 15, 1348, in response to an inquiry from the mayor of nearby Strasbourg, France, who sought evidence of Jews poisoning local wells.

"We have received your gracious letters with pleasure, and have accordingly sent you in writing under our seal the confessions made by a Jew called Bona Dies. He was condemned to be set on the wheel, where he survived for four days and nights. While he could still speak he held unvaryingly to his first story. And we have informed you that in the lordship of the Count of Savoy many Jews, and Christians as well, have confessed to the same appalling crime. Accordingly they were condemned to punishment by burning and impalement. The confessions they made have been communicated to our friends the officials and councillors of Bern and Fribourg at their request."

the plague. Some may have had other motives that had more to do with the financial situation of Jews than with the disease. Observed Jacob Twinger, a contemporary chronicler: "If the Jews had been poor, and rulers of other countries had not been in their debt, they would never have been burnt."[90]

Whatever the cause of the outbreaks of violence, all too often local authorities did little or nothing to stem the slaughter. Sometimes they were intimidated by the mobs. On other occasions they shared the mindless prejudice of the killers and took part in the killings themselves.

Not all Europeans turned against the Jews. In England, for example, Jews were blamed for the Black Death but were not persecuted. And here and there a few sympathetic nobles and government administrators did what they could to stop the mobs. In Lithuania and Poland, for instance, royal authorities offered Jews asylum and protected them.

Jews were not the only victims of fear and hysteria, though. Crazed mobs also attacked nobles, strangers from other countries, lepers, Gypsies, and witches. In Spain, Christians killed Arab Muslims who were suspected of being hired by Jews to carry out acts of poisoning.

The church finally intervened in the frenzied killing of Jews in 1348, when medical faculties at Paris and Montpellier concluded that Jews had not caused the plague.

The Pope Speaks Out

Upon hearing of the mob attacks against the Jews, Pope Clement VI spoke out in their defense with these words, which are recorded in Abba Eban's book *Heritage: Civilization and the Jews*.

"Since this pestilence is all but universal everywhere, and by a mysterious decree of God has afflicted, and continues to afflict, both Jews and many other nations throughout the diverse regions of the earth to whom a common existence with Jews is unknown, [the charge] that Jews have provided the cause or the occasion for such a crime is without plausibility."

In response, on July 5, 1348, Pope Clement VI called for an end to the murders. He ordered Christians "Not to dare . . . to capture, strike, wound or kill any Jews or expel them from their service."[91]

But the pope's words did little to halt the massacres, for the need to blame and punish someone for the sufferings inflicted by the Black Death proved too great to be stopped by anyone. By 1351 Christian mobs had destroyed 60 major European communities of Jews and 150 smaller ones. Altogether as many as 350 different acts of mass slaughter took place. And none of these gruesome killings saved anyone from the Black Death.

Help, Hope, and Healing

As the Black Death rapidly demolished vast populations of humanity, Europeans desperately sought help from the two institutions that traditionally provided them with hope and healing—the medical profession and the Catholic Church. Despite heroic attempts by many individual physicians and priests, neither institution had any success. Doctors were unable to heal victims or prevent others from catching the Black Death. Baffled by the onslaught of the Great Mortality, church officials offered little but words of comfort to those who perished or watched their loved ones die.

Human ignorance was a major cause of these failings. Medieval medicine was steeped in tradition, superstition, and false information when the Black Death struck. The Catholic

Medieval townspeople dance and pray to God to bring an end to the devastating plague.

Church was partly to blame, too; its restrictions on scientific research and the expression of new ideas stifled progress in efforts to understand human health. In 1300, for instance, the pope banned the practice of dissecting human cadavers, a decision that kept physicians ignorant about basic anatomy and the impact of disease on the human body.

Stuck in the Past

Europe's physicians—many of whom rarely even touched their patients—kept themselves in ignorance by accepting without question the theories of ancient thinkers. The ideas of Galen, a Greek physician and writer during the second century A.D., guided European and Islamic medicine for more than a thousand years.

Galen's ideas about medicine dominated popular medical practices during the Middle Ages.

One of Galen's now-discredited theories held that the universe was made up of four basic qualities: warmth, wetness, dryness, and coldness. He believed that good health was determined by a balance of four basic fluids, or humors, in the human body. Galen identified these as blood, phlegm, and two types of bile—one black, the other yellow. As British author Jonathan Miller explains,

> Blood corresponded to air and expressed the combined qualities of heat and wetness; phlegm duplicated the element of water, since it was cold and wet: yellow bile or choler corresponded to the dry heat of fire, while cold dryness of earth was represented by black bile or melancholy.[92]

According to Galen, human illness resulted when there was an imbalance of these humors. To many medieval thinkers, Galen's idea about humors explained why some people caught the plague and others did not. The solution was to use medical treatments that restored a state of equilibrium. If a patient's body seemed to be too hot, for example, then a doctor should prescribe certain foods that would make the patient's body cooler. Other foods should be consumed, however, if the patient's flesh were too cool.

Galen never actually prescribed these treatments for the plague, and his volume entitled *Book of Fevers* did not offer much information on how to treat someone stricken with pestilence. Nonetheless, the book was the only one used by most medieval doctors, so they adapted Galen's remedies in the desperate struggle against the Black Death.

They also tried a variety of other treatments. Many aggressively attacked the buboes, which they thought were the centers of the disease. One way to do this was to apply dried toads directly on top of the boils.

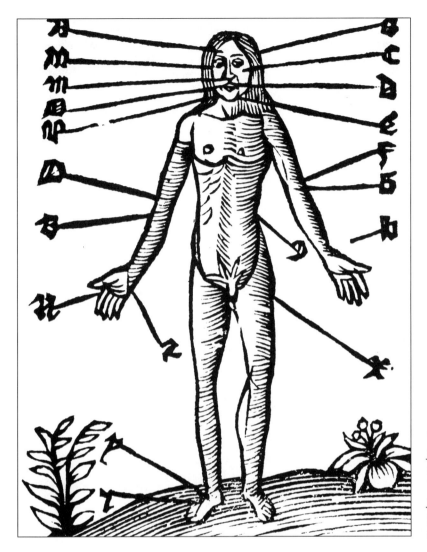

This bloodletting guide is from an early sixteenth-century reference manual. The lines leading to the figure's body indicate points from which blood is to be let.

These shriveled creatures were expected to soak up plague poisons from the patients.

Some physicians burned the swellings with a hot iron. Others sliced them open with a thin sharp blade and released foul greenish pus and what they believed to be evil vapors. Next, they rubbed special poultices made from violets or various other ingredients directly into wounds to heal the damaged tissue. During this ordeal, patients tried to make themselves stronger and more resistant to the disease by drinking moderate amounts of fruit juices.

Bleeding was also used. This was done by cutting open a vein in the arm and letting the blood drip into an open container. The veins that were bled during this procedure were believed to have astrological connections with heavenly bodies. The correct amount of bloodletting supposedly balanced the humors in one's body and helped ward off pestilence. Another method was cupping—an operation done with a heated glass vessel to draw blood to the surface of the skin.

Help, Hope, and Healing

A Preventative to Death?

This extract from Robert S. Gottfried's *The Black Death: Natural and Human Disaster in Medieval Europe* reveals a fourteenth-century recipe for a medicinal preventative to the Black Death.

"A medicine for the pestilence. Take five cups of [the herb] rue if it be a man, and if it be a woman leave out the rue, for rue is a restorative to a man and wasting to a woman; and then take thereto five crops of [the herb] tansey and five little blades of [the flower] columbine, and a great quantity of marigold flowers full of the small chives from the crops that are like saffron chives. And if you may not get the flowers, take the leaves, and then you must have of the marigolds more than the others. Then take an egg that is newly laid, and make a hole in either end, and blow out all that is within. And lay it to the fire and let it roast till it may be ground to powder, but do not burn it. Then take a quantity of good treacle [a medicinal syrup], and bray all these herbs therin with good ale, but do not strain them. And then make the sick drink it for three evenings and three mornings. If they [the sick] hold it, they shall have life."

Not all treatments were invasive. Many doctors also made use of herbal ointments and salves as curative medicines. Some were pleasant, soothing potions consisting of apple, syrup, rosewater, peppermint, and lemon. Others were exotic concoctions that often contained ingredients such as powdered stag's horn, snake meat, powdered emeralds, liquid gold, and various toxic substances.

All too soon, doctors and physicians discovered that none of these treatments worked. Few of their efforts to prevent the spread of the disease worked either—though not for lack of trying.

Prevention

Doctors and priests alike advised patients and parishioners to seek protection from God. Medieval doctors routinely asked patients if they had confessed their sins and received communion—acts that could win them salvation. In the case of the Black Death, doctors also recommended the wearing of charms as preventatives. Across Europe many Christians wore small crosses about their necks, while their Muslim counterparts in the Mideast, North Africa, and elsewhere carried replicas of gold lions.

Prayer was held out as the surest method of prevention. Among the more popular prayers is this one, which mixes Christian beliefs and astrology to persuade heaven to cancel the evil influence of plague-causing stars:

Star of Heaven, who nourished the Lord and rooted up the plague of death which our first parents planted; may that star now deign to counter the constellations whose strife brings the people the ulcers of a terrible death. O glorious star of the sea, save us from the plague. Hear us: for your Son who honours you denies you nothing. Jesus, save us, for whom the Virgin Mary prays to you.[93]

In addition to prayer, purification of the air was recommended as a preventative measure. Many people believed that stagnant air contained infections. The solution was to stir up the air to keep it clean. Cannon explosions, gunfire, and pealing church bells rang out from sunrise to sunset in many towns and villages across Europe as frightened men and women tried to stimulate the flow of air in their communities. According to Johannes Nohl,

> Many people had little birds flying about in their rooms so that they might absorb the poison and keep the air in motion. It was also believed that spiders, particularly the larger and speckled species, absorbed all poisons in the houses, thus preserving the inhabitants from infection.[94]

Many people also placed bowls of milk and pieces of freshly baked bread impaled on wooden sticks inside their homes to absorb any plague poisons that drifted inside.

A plague doctor, in clothing worn to protect him from disease.

The burning of fires offered another means of purifying the air of bad agents. As an extra precaution, many people burned sweet smelling woods such as juniper, ash, oak, and pine in their cook fires. At Avignon, France, Pope Clement VI, under orders from his doctor, spent his days and nights sitting between two fireplaces as the Black Death raged through the city. Whether owing to his isolation or to the fires that may have destroyed any fleas in the room, the pope successfully avoided getting the plague.

Since many medical authorities argued that sweet, fragrant smells created beneficial agents that counteracted the disease, those living in dread of the plague often kept fragrant flowers nearby. Women were considered by their doctors to be especially at risk and often clutched a small flower bouquet to their noses whenever they left their homes.

Some people wore masks to avoid breathing foul air. In Rome, plague physicians became known as "beak doctors" because of the oversized birdlike masks they wore to protect themselves from their dying patients.

Physicians also advised staying indoors at night and darkening any well-lit windows to ward off approaching foul air. Rest was thought to be a good idea, but people were urged not to get too much sleep, especially in the daytime. Nor should they sleep on their backs, for such a position only made entrance of foul air into the nostrils and lungs all that much easier. Instead, doctors advised people to lie on one side and move often in bed during the night.

Dionysius Colle, a fourteenth-century physician, urged people to also avoid foul-smelling places such as latrines and charnel houses—places where bodies or bones were deposited.

But other doctors disagreed. Arguing that "bad" would drive out "bad," they advised

Help, Hope, and Healing **61**

their patients to bathe in small amounts of urine and to breathe the stench of latrines as a means of fumigating against the Black Death. Some even recommended bathing in and drinking goat urine. In the Crimea region along the Black Sea, people threw dead dogs into the streets to stink out the agents of pestilence. Others kept stinking billy goats in their houses.

Changing Personal Habits

Most doctors were far more apt to recommend cleanliness, a proper diet, and clean living as the best way to avoid the plague. However, their views differed widely on how best to do this. Some recommended, for example, the washing of hands and feet, but not entire bodies. By washing the entire body, they said, patients would cause skin pores to widen and be more receptive to corrupted air.

Active people were thought to be at greater risk than inactive people. Fatigue was to be avoided at all costs. Passionate and highly emotional people, athletes, and anyone who led vigorous physical lives were strongly admonished to reduce their level of activity. Instead, they were urged to move slowly and avoid exercise, especially if they felt illness coming upon them.

Proper diet was also considered an important preventative measure. Only light meals were recommended, and they were to be chewed carefully and thoroughly. Foods that spoiled quickly, such as meat and dairy products, were to be shunned. According to a report from the University of Paris medical faculty in 1348, "No poultry should be eaten, no waterfowl, no suckling pig, no old beef, altogether no fat meat. . . . Olive oil with food is mortal [deadly]." [95] Medical experts also frowned on eating desserts. John of Burgundy, an English medical practitioner in 1365, offered these comprehensive, preventative measures:

> First you should avoid over-indulgence in food and drink, and also avoid baths and everything which might rarefy the body and open the pores, for the pores are the doorways through which poisonous air can enter, piercing the heart and corrupting the life force. Above all sexual intercourse should be avoided. You should eat little or no fruit, unless it is sour, and should consume easily-digested food and spice wine diluted with water. Avoid mead and everything else made with honey, and season food with strong vinegar. [96]

The Beak Doctors

These rhymed verses, excerpted from Johannes Nohl's *The Black Death: A Chronicle of the Plague Compiled from Contemporary Sources*, depict the strange appearances of the "beak doctors" who wore outlandish clothes and bizarre birdlike masks to protect themselves from the Black Death.

> As may be seen on picture here,
> In Rome the doctors do appear,
> When to their patients they are called,
> In places by the plague appalled,
> Their hats and cloaks, of fashion new,
> Are made of oilcloth, dark of hue,
> Their caps with glasses are designed,
> Their bills with antidotes all lined,
> That foulsome air may do no harm,
> Nor cause the doctor man alarm
> The staff in hand must serve to show
> Their noble trade where'er they go.

In an attempt to escape the disease, townspeople fled to the country.

On the other hand, doctors recommended beneficial antiplague meals that consisted of bread, eggs, nuts, and fruit consumed in small amounts. Wine and water were the best drinks to have with meals.

Special herbal remedies were also popular in the fourteenth century. Apothecaries—specialists in herbal remedies—dug through their stores of plants to find those that might stave off infection. Forerunners of the modern pharmacists, these herbalists used their knowledge of plants to provide a variety of medicines, both curatives and preventatives.

They recommended that anyone wishing to escape the Black Death should cultivate a small garden of myrrh, saffron, pepper, onion, garlic, and leeks—spices and herbs believed to ward off disease if consumed. They also urged the eating of figs, the woody herb rue, and filbert nuts.

The right frame of mind was also considered to be an important way of warding off the Black Death. Inhabitants of many medieval societies wracked by the plague were encouraged to keep up their spirits and have a positive outlook on life. They were told to avoid morbid thoughts despite the death and dying taking place around them. A mind that dwelled on death only invited death; one that focused on pleasant things brought on good health. As two Italian physicians, known as Marsilio and Garbo, pointed out:

No man should think of death. . . . Nothing should distress him, but all his thoughts should be directed to pleasing, agreeable and delicious things. . . . Beautiful landscapes, fine gardens should be visited. . . . Listening to beautiful, melodious songs is wholesome, as is also to enjoy the joys of the fine season in the company of agreeable people. The contemplation of gold and silver and other precious stones is comforting to the heart.[97]

Stronger Measures

Medieval medicine also offered certain procedures and surgical measures that were supposed to help prevent the spread of the plague. Some physicians prescribed special laxatives and diuretics to purge people of waste fluids that might carry the Black Death. Many also believed that bleeding offered both cure and prevention.

Burning or cutting the skin to form blisters was another popular preventative measure. Patients kept the blisters from closing during the healing process by applying layers of butter or lard to them. This process continued until the Black Death no longer presented a threat.

In the end, however, neither preventative measures nor cures made any difference. Most of the Black Death's victims died. And the small percentage who survived the disease most likely did so despite their physicians' best efforts.

These attempts had some value, though, suggests historian Philip Ziegler: "Essentially they were a morale building exercise; the morale of the physicians in that they made him feel at least remotely in control of the situation, and of the patient, in that they offered a slight hope of escape from death."[98]

By far the best advice any doctor could offer was that people should run away from the disease. The importance of taking flight was immortalized in a piece of verse called "Three Adverb Pills" by Rhasis, the famous Arabian physician who influenced many medieval doctors:

> Three things by which each simple man
> From plague escape and sickness can,
> Start soon, flee far from town or land
> On which the plague has laid its hand,
> Return but late to such a place
> Where pestilence has stayed its pace.[99]

Those who tried to flee followed a preset route that, if taken, promised greater preventative power. People were to avoid low elevations, coastal areas, swamps, stagnant water, and shelters that had southern exposures. Instead, they should seek cool, dry areas, preferably in the mountains.

The Limited Abilities of Doctors

Despite their feeble medical abilities, many dedicated physicians remained with their pa-

tients until they, too, were struck down. In Venice, for example, approximately twenty out of twenty-four doctors may have perished from the disease.

But all too often physicians took their own advice and fled. Their abandonment of their patients, plus their apparent medical incompetence, brought them dishonor and ridicule across Europe. "The plague was shameful for the physicians, who could give no help at all, especially as, out of fear of infection, they hesitated to visit the sick,"[100] complained Guy de Chauliac, the pope's personal physician.

Giovanni Boccaccio's description of doctors in Florence summed up the attitude of many Europeans: "Either the disease was such that no treatment was possible or the doctors were so ignorant that they did not know what caused it, and consequently could not administer the proper remedy."[101]

Few people in the fourteenth century had great confidence in the ability of the medical practitioners in the first place. Instead, they put their greatest hope and faith in their religious leaders.

Fear and Honor in the Clergy

Everywhere in Europe terrified Christians turned to their local priests and bishops for guidance, comfort, reassurance, and hope. In response, religious leaders offered prayers and religious vows to fight the plague. Their weapons had little effect. As the number of dead multiplied, the clergy's greatest duty was to prepare Christians for death and the afterlife. One of their biggest tasks was to perform last rites for an ever-growing number of plague victims. This ritual required priests to annoint a dying person and to say special prayers for his or her salvation. Afterward, the priest was expected to conduct a Christian funeral for the dead.

Like their medical counterparts, many priests acted heroically and performed their duties honorably even though it meant that thousands died within their own ranks. Others worried more about their own survival than the spiritual comfort of others. In France and Germany, for example, many priests stood apart from the dying and provided the communion wafer of bread to them on a long pole or a long-handled spoon to avoid being infected. Others, meanwhile, fled the ravaging Black Death. Their absence, along with a high number of deaths among the clergy, resulted in a critical shortage of priests. This scarcity became so acute that the pope had no choice but to relax church rules and allow women and other laypeople within the church to perform priestly duties such as hearing confessions and carrying out last rites.

Acts of Piety

Many Christians also performed other acts of piety. They hoped these deeds would appease God's wrath and make the plague disappear. Under the leadership of church officials, they erected new churches, pillars, statues, and altars to honor God, Jesus, and the Virgin Mary. They also honored many saints, including St. Sebastian, Rose of Viterbo, Domencia de Paradisco, and St. Rock of Montpellier, and cried out to them for protection from the ravages of the Black Death.

Many groups of terrified Christians made pilgrimages to places such as Messina, Italy, just to be near the shrines or graves of certain saints. Pilgrims often dug up the remains of saints because they believed that relics such as a skull or a piece of bone offered them spiritual protection from the plague. These bone fragments were so highly sought after that they became commodities on the black market. Many rich Europeans tried to buy as many relics as they could to guarantee their safety.

In Vienna, one group of Christians attended religious services and passed among themselves silver arrows that had touched another arrow believed to have killed St. Sebastian. According to Nohl, they also took communion by drinking sacramental wine "which had previously passed through the

A Prayer for Help

This popular prayer to St. Sebastian, an Italian martyr, for protection from the Black Death is extracted from Rosemary Horrox's *The Black Death*.

"O St Sebastian, guard and defend me, morning and evening, every minute of every hour, while I am still of sound mind; and, Martyr, diminish the strength of that vile illness called an epidemic which is threatening me. Protect and keep me and all my friends from this plague. We put our trust in God and St Mary, and in you, O holy Martyr. You, citizen of Milan, could through God's power, halt this pestilence if you chose. For it is known to many that you have that merit. . . . O martyr Sebastian! Be with us always, and by your merits keep us safe and sound and protected from plague. Commend us to the Trinity and to the Virgin Mary, so that when we die we may have our reward: to behold God in the company of martyrs."

skull of the . . . [saint] . . . and a particle of the bone of the arm was offered to be kissed. All this as a preservative against infection."[102]

Along with pilgrimages, Christians also obeyed the pope's command to fill the streets with devout processions to openly demonstrate their piety and boost the spirits of

Many Christians prayed to Italian martyr St. Sebastian for protection against the Black Death.

Christians as the Black Death rampaged across Europe. Many Christians believed that they could move closer to God and boost their spirituality by appearing to be humble and poor. Barefooted, dressed in sack cloths, and covered with ashes, they paraded through town streets, ripped at their hair and clothes, and prayed to God to save them from the plague.

These demonstrators generated a great deal of attention throughout Europe. In time, however, they were overshadowed by an even larger mass movement that had neither the urging nor the blessing of the pope.

The Flagellants

This movement consisted of people who were often called cross brethren or cross brothers. Most Europeans knew them as flagellants. For the most part, they were religious zealots who belonged to a massive crusade that first arose to prominence in Germany. They then swept into France and the Low Countries (what is now Belgium, Luxembourg, and the Netherlands) and later, during the period of the Black Death, moved into eastern Europe. Representing all social classes of medieval society, flagellants believed they could stop the Black Death by performing public acts of penance for their sins. Some flagellants interpreted the Black Death as a portent of coming supernatural events. Brothers of the Cross in Germany, for example, believed a long dead hero, Emperor Frederick Barbarosa, would come back to life and save them from the Black Death. Others thought Jesus Christ would soon appear.

Often numbering more than forty thousand, the flagellants walked from town to town like a huge army. Dressed in black robes with cowled hoods and a felt hat that covered

A Fourteenth-Century Surgeon Explains His Craft

In this passage, excerpted from John R. Green's *Medical History for Students*, Guy de Chauliac (1300–1368), a doctor who chronicled the Black Death, provides modern readers with a glimpse into the philosophy of fourteenth-century surgery.

"The conditions necessary for the Surgeon are four: First, he should be learned; Second, he should be expert; Third, he must be ingenious; Fourth, he should be able to adapt himself.

It is required for the First that the Surgeon should know not only the principles of surgery, but also those of medicine in theory and practice; for the Second, that he should have seen others operate; for the Third, that he should be ingenious, of good judgment and memory to recognize conditions; and for the Fourth, that he be adaptable and able to accommodate himself to circumstance.

Let the Surgeon be bold in all sure things and fearful in dangerous things; let him avoid all faulty treatments and practices. He ought to be gracious to the sick, considerate to his associates, cautious in his prognostications. Let him be modest, dignified, gentle, pitiful, and merciful; not covetous, nor an extortionist of money; but rather let his reward be according to his work, to the means of the patient, to the quality of the issue, and to his own dignity."

---

their eyes, they carried wooden crosses and chanted religious hymns. At night, they bore torches and candles as they moved across the cobblestoned streets. Striding in pairs, their eyes fixed on the earth, the flagellants solemnly marched in a serpentlike parade through the streets and recited these words:

> Whoe'er to save his soul is fain,
> Must pay and render back again.
> His safety so shall he consult;
> Help us, good Lord, to this result.[103]

They halted only when they reached the town square or wherever the main church was located. Inside the church, they stripped to their underclothes and returned to the churchyard with whips called *flagella*. Each whip consisted of a stick with three knotted leather thongs pierced by small iron nails. Under the guidance of an experienced leader, the men

flogged themselves across their naked backs with the whips until blood dripped down their legs. A chronicler in Gottingen, Germany, observed, "I have seen when they whipped themselves, how sometimes those bits of metal penetrated the flesh so deeply that it took more than two attempts to pull them out."[104]

As the flagellants lashed themselves, they sang religious songs and chanted verses like these:

> Come here for penance good and well,
> Thus we escape from burning hell.
> Lucifer's a wicked wight,
> His prey he sets with pitch alight. . . .
> Jesus was refreshed with gall
> We, therefore, on our cross now fall.[105]

At this point, they fell one at a time on the ground and with outstretched arms and legs made the shape of a cross and cried out for forgiveness for their personal sins. Then they made different shapes with their body, each one symbolizing a particular sin. Lying on one side with three fingers stretched out past the head meant the person atoned for the sin of perjury. An adulterer lay on his stomach; a murderer positioned himself on his back.

Life among the flagellants was hard. They engaged in ritual self-punishment three times a day—twice in public, once in private—in an attempt to appease God and bring about an end to the Black Death. They slept on straw under a small blanket. Men seldom washed or shaved their beards. Their food was simple. Mingling with women was forbidden. Accepting charity during their pilgrimage was forbidden.

Huge crowds greeted them wherever they appeared and generally received them with great respect. Many people came to watch the flogging and the public display of piety because they considered the flagellants true holy men who had the power to thwart the mortality of the plague. Other spectators, however, were bemused by the thousands of scantily dressed men wounding themselves with barbs and singing hymns. To them, the spectacle of public penance was merely a temporary distraction from the everyday terror of the Black Death.

Flagellants, however, were deadly serious. And as the plague grew worse, the more fanatical among their ranks turned increasingly violent. Upon their arrival at many

The flagellants, or cross brethren, believed the plague could be stopped by performing public acts of penance for sins.

How the Flagellants Demonstrated

Chronicler Heinrich of Herford's graphic description of how the flagellants scourged themselves to appease God is found in Johannes Nohl's *The Black Death: A Chronicle of the Plague Compiled from Contemporary Sources.*

"Each scourge was a kind of stick from which three tails with large knots hung down. Right through the knots iron spikes as sharp as needles were thrust which penetrated about the length of a grain of wheat or a little more beyond the knots. With such scourges they beat themselves on their naked bodies so that they became swollen and blue, the blood ran down to the ground and bespattered the walls of the churches in which they scourged themselves. Occasionally they drove the spikes so deep into the flesh that they could only be pulled out by a second wrench."

towns, extremists incited anti-Jewish hysteria and led murderous attacks on local Jews.

Government and church officials reacted with alarm as the actions of the flagellants became bolder and more menacing. Finally, in 1349, the church clamped down on the flagellants. Fearing they had usurped the Catholic Church's authority to lead religious observance, Pope Clement II publicly condemned all flagellants. He threatened them with excommunication if they did not disband. At the same time, various European kings, nobles, and government leaders also cracked down on the cross brethren by sending in troops to disperse them. Under such pressure, the movement faded away within a year of the pope's proclamation.

A Tragic Legacy

But the flagellants left behind a tragic legacy. Because of their unsanitary, bloody practices; their ability to draw large crowds of spectators; and their movement of great numbers of people from one place to the next, they helped to spread the very disease that they had hoped to end.

The failure of the flagellant movement only added to the terrifying and inescapable conclusion that human beings had not a single means of protection from the monster known as the Black Death. It would run its course unimpeded. But what would the earth be like when the pestilence finished inflicting its horror?

CHAPTER 6

An Altered Way of Life

By 1352 the worst of the Black Death was over. But its impact would last for centuries. The disease had disrupted European civilization with the destructiveness and ferocity of a massive and devastating war. Every aspect of society was permanently altered in some way by the onslaught of the disease. Thousands of European towns and villages lay silenced and abandoned. Manors and small farms were in ruins. Crops rotted in the fields. Churches and monasteries were empty; universities and halls of government were shut down. Banks and businesses went bankrupt. Common graves stretched across the countryside. Vultures, crows, rats, and flies feasted on unburied corpses.

This was the world left to the living. As if this were not bad enough, survivors faced one additional problem: widespread hunger. Few livestock had survived the devastation of the foregoing years. In addition, vast crops of

grains and vegetables remained unattended because too few workers remained. Unusually cold, wet weather continued to make agriculture difficult.

One of the most terrifying new realities facing Europeans was the permanence of the plague in their lives. Though the epidemic was over, the disease did not disappear. Instead, it settled into Europe and recurred as epidemics in 1361, 1363, 1369, 1371, 1390, 1405, and several times afterward, though never with the intensity of the Black Death. Author Charles L. Mee Jr. argues that

> the recurrence of the plague after people thought the worst was over may have been the most devastating development of all. In short, Europe was swept not only by a bacillus but also by a widespread psychic breakdown—by abject terror, panic, rage, vengefulness, cringing remorse, selfish-

A fifteenth-century illustration shows God looking out from the clouds over a group of plague victims.

ness, hysteria, and above all, by an over-whelming sense of powerlessness in the face of an inescapable horror.[106]

The appalling spectacle of losing one out of every three people shook the religious beliefs of most Christians. Many believed that the Black Death flourished because God was angry over the sinful ways of humanity. As a result, many faithful Christians worked hard to avoid another catastrophe. Gifts to charities, hospitals, and cathedrals continued even after the worst of the disease was over. Religious pilgrimages to holy sites and cathedrals begun during the plague also continued. So many pilgrims filled the roads of Europe, in fact, that popular writers of the second half of the fourteenth century made money selling travel books that offered advice on where to eat and sleep.

Question of Faith

Not everyone became more pious in the wake of the plague. Many Christians were disillusioned with the Catholic Church because it apparently failed them. They could not understand why God had ignored their prayers to stop the plague. Nor could they accept that the priests had not warned them that this incomprehensible killer was coming. Resentment was also strong over the fact that many priests deserted their flocks once the plague arrived and abandoned the dying without administering the necessary rituals to prepare Catholics for death. Some people even claimed that priests charged more money for their services during the plague. All these complaints reflected a dark and brooding spirit that haunted many Europeans and caused them to find answers elsewhere.

Some people turned to new interpretations of Christianity. Religious reformer John

A Turn for the Worse?

Sir Arthur Bryant's *The Age of Chivalry* contains this assessment of human nature made by William Dene, a chronicler in Rochester, England, during the immediate aftermath of the Black Death.

"The people for the greater part ever became more depraved, more prone to every vice and more inclined than before to evil and wickedness, not thinking of death nor of the past plague nor of their own salvation. . . . Priests, little weighing the sacrifice of a contrite spirit, betook themselves to where they could get larger stipends than in their own benefices, on which account many benefices remained unserved. Day by day, the dangers to souls both in clergy and people multiplied. . . . The labourers and skilled workmen were imbued with such a spirit of rebellion that neither king, law nor justice could curb them."

Wycliffe in England and Bohemia's John Huss, along with other activists, openly challenged church authority and many of its teachings. Wycliffe, for example, translated the Bible into English so that his countrymen could read it for themselves rather than having to rely on the authority of Catholic officials. He also expressed doubt that consecrated bread eaten during communion actually became the flesh of Christ, as Catholic priests claimed. These rumblings, plus many others, set the stage for a religious revolution called the Protestant Reformation—a movement of the early sixteenth century that was based on the idea that men and women had a direct relationship with God and did not need priests, bishops, or popes to intervene on their behalf.

Religious reformer John Wycliffe publicly expressed doubts about Catholicism, setting the stage for the Protestant Reformation.

Some disenchanted Christians abandoned Christianity altogether and joined various new cults that championed beliefs ranging from free thinking to mysticism. Among the more extreme of the new groups were the Luciferians, a cult that believed God took over the throne of heaven through the use of force.

Weakened by defections from the ranks of believers, the Catholic Church also suffered a severe shortage of clergy. The church found replacements for the dead and runaway priests, but the shortage of qualified candidates meant that many of the new recruits were less pious, less educated, and less devoted than their predecessors. They were also less likely than previous generations to read and speak Latin—the official language of the church. In its weakened state, the church and all of its traditions, including the use of Latin, carried less authority. For these reasons, priests and other church officials increasingly used their own native tongues rather than Latin to impart Catholic teachings and perform rituals. As a result, Europe witnessed the rise in importance of everyday languages such as Italian, French, English, and German and a decline in the once dominant use of Latin.

A Rise in Immorality

An enfeebled and discredited church could do little to check a sudden rise of immorality following the Black Death. Massive horror, despair, grief, and loss of religious faith caused many survivors of the Black Death to be more cynical, pessimistic, and fearful and less virtuous than before. The Becchini, the flagellants, and countless others from all walks of life who acted selfishly and irresponsibly during the crisis revealed many shocking examples of human nature at its worst. Though most Europeans were disgusted with such barbaric behavior, many also wondered why anyone should obey the old medieval laws and customs. After all, they reasoned, the Black Death might return any day and repeat its indiscriminate killing. What was the point of clinging to a way of life that no longer existed? According to historian Robert S. Gottfried,

> People were traumatized. They lost faith in their own abilities, in the old values, and if not in God then in the traditional ways in which He had been propitiated. Europe was plunged into a moral crisis. The old order was collapsing and the new one was not yet in place.[107]

The plague had also proved that human life was precarious, fragile, and often brief. From this experience many concluded that they should live for the moment. Why not fend for themselves, indulge in the glut of material things left behind by the dead, and ignore the needs of neighbors and community, they wondered. Such attitudes made all attempts at rebuilding society extremely difficult. One French chronicler observed that

> people were afterwards more avaricious and grasping, even when they possessed more of the goods of this world than before. They were more covetous, vexing themselves by contentious quarrels, strifes and law-suits. . . . Ignorance, was rampant.[108]

Even many Catholic priests, who were trained to shun the material things of the world, fell victim to temptation, especially when they were confronted with the excessive financial contributions many Christians gave to the church. A monk in Westminster, England, known as John of Reading, wrote that desire for wealth

> wounded the regular clergy very much. . . . The superfluous wealth poured their way, through confessions and bequests, in such quantities that they . . . [forgot their vows of poverty and] lusted after things of the world and of the flesh, not of heaven.[109]

The moral breakdown and the collapse of law and order also gave rise to increased violence in parts of Europe during the years immediately following the Black Death. Bands of robbers and killers menaced Europeans

Great Is My Envy of You

Like millions of others, the Italian diplomat and poet Petrarch grieved over the loss of loved ones taken by the plague. In this famous poem, which appears in editor Maynard Mack's *The Continental Edition of World Masterpieces*, the famous poet laments the death of his beloved Laura, who perished at Avignon, France.

Great is my envy of you, earth,
   in your greed
Folding her in invisible embrace
Denying me the look of the sweet face
Where I found peace from all
   my strife at need!

Great is my envy of heaven
   which can lead

And lock within itself in avarice
That spirit from its lovely biding-place
And leave so many others here to bleed!

Great is my envy of those souls
   whose reward
Is the gentle heaven of her company,
Which I so fiercely sought beneath
   these skies!

Great is my envy of death whose curt
   hard sword
Carried her whom I called my
   life away;
Me he disdains, and mocks me from
   her eyes!

everywhere. Killings multiplied. For example, the murder rate from 1349 to 1369 in England was twice that of the years between 1320 to 1347.

Sometimes violence even broke out against the clergy. An angry mob attacked monks near a cathedral in Worcester in 1349. Such discontent only grew worse over the next few years. In 1381 a gang of rebels cut off the head of Simon Sudbury, the archbishop of Canterbury in London, as a large crowd of onlookers applauded and cheered.

Post-plague artists often focused their works on that of the dead. Here, a miniature from The Book of Hours, *entitled* Doctor Death.

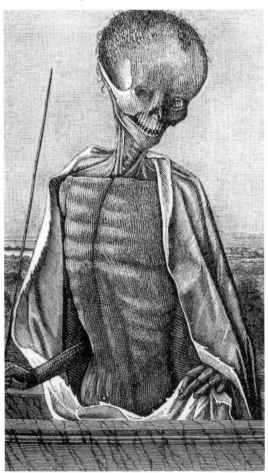

Fixed on the Macabre

An increase in violence was not the only visible change in human behavior in the postplague days. Many people also became fixated on the macabre. Death became a fascination and obsession for many troubled survivors of the Black Death. Before the Great Pestilence, most Europeans generally accepted death as a sad but normal event in human affairs. But now people of all ages dwelled on the idea as never before. "Funerals became festivals, the greatest event of a lifetime,"[110] writes historian Gottfried. Images of death and horror became common in religious art, too. For example, European artists created funeral brasses and tombs that bore images of rotting cadavers being eaten by toads, worms, and birds of prey. Others showed skeletons with snakes wrapped around them. Religious paintings, meanwhile, featured scenes of devils flailing doomed corpses.

Many artists of the time captured postplague fears and attitudes in a symbolic "Dance of Death." Images of "Death" dancing with living human beings appeared in many forms. Murals, for example, appeared on many church walls with depictions of Death as a fearful being called the Grim Reaper. Joined by skeletons, the Grim Reaper danced with human beings of various ages and social standings to emphasize that death comes to all people and can strike any time—just as the Black Death did.

Though death had long existed as a theme in literature, it received extraordinary attention in the wake of the Black Death. An example of this is the fourteenth-century poem "It Is Good to Think on Death." Written by an anonymous poet, the story told by the poem takes place "in the season of huge mortality, of sundry disease, with the pestilence heavily

One of the many "Dance of Death" illustrations, popular in post-plague Europe.

reigning"[111] and features an imaginary debate between the corpse of a once beautiful woman and the worms that are eating it. The opening lines of the poem serve as an epitaph for the woman, as revealed in this prose retelling:

> Look at my image and see how I was once fresh and gay, who am now turned to worms' meat and corruption; just foul earth, stinking slime and clay. Pay attention to the disputation written here and inscribe it upon your heart so you may learn some wisdom from studying it, and realize what you are and what you shall become. When you least expect it death comes to conquer you. While your grave is still undug it is good to think on death.[112]

Humanity was not always morose after the plague subsided. Survivors were also happy to be alive. But their delight was tempered, if not twisted, by the horror they had personally witnessed. Johannes Nohl observes that, after the plague, "a wanton joy of life had come over humanity. On festive occasions the people were not content with expressing their joy, but jeered and railed at death."[113] This attitude was dramatized in a new ceremony that arose in parts of Germany. Once a year, town residents marched in a parade and symbolically drove Death from their city gates. Crowds of young people also flaunted death in the graveyards of Europe. Here, among tombstones and mausoleums, they held parties, danced, feasted, and played games. The Catholic Church watched these social gatherings with growing alarm and concluded that they were unwholesome and sacrilegious. At last, in 1394 the pope put an end to them when he threatened excommunication to any person who tried "to dance, fight, throw iron or wood bars, to play with wheels, to bowl, or play dice or other unseemly games or commit other unseemly acts upon the graves of the dead."[114]

An Altered Way of Life

Depopulation

In 1351 a staff of researchers for the pope reported that an estimated 24 million Europeans had lost their lives during the onslaught of the Black Death. This massive death toll caused great transformations in Europe. Among them were dramatic physical changes. Thousands of abandoned homes and manors dotted Europe. Entire villages and towns ceased to exist. In England alone an estimated thirteen hundred villages became ghost towns from 1350 to 1500.

Most communities struck by the Great Pestilence lost anywhere from 25 to 40 percent of their local populations. In some settlements, so few villagers were left that those who remained had no choice but to leave.

Inside abandoned dwellings lay vast amounts of money, gold, silver, precious gems, clothing, and other material possessions. These sometimes fell into the hands of friends and relatives; other times, perfect strangers laid claim to these items. Historian Barbara W. Tuchman offers this description of how property of Europe's dead often changed hands: "The poor moved into empty houses, slept on beds, and ate off silver. Peasants acquired unclaimed tools and livestock, even a wine press, forge, or mill left without owners, and other possessions they never had before."[115]

The net effect of this large-scale transfer of wealth enabled many poor Europeans to become richer than they ever before dreamed.

Even the age mix of the people changed. Though people of all ages were struck down by the plague, people of various age groups did not die in equal numbers. When the Black Death struck, the very young and the very old were among the first to die. But when the disease returned in 1361, it killed an even higher percentage of young people. This

may have occurred because older Europeans had acquired immunities when the Black Death struck during their youth and were less likely to die when the plague returned. Whatever the reason, some regions were left with older populations than would usually be found in medieval Europe.

There was also an economic loss associated with the deaths of so many young people. Their deaths squandered precious resources, as historian David Herlitly observes:

The wealth and effort invested in the rearing of children remained in significant measure wasted. Death ruthlessly thinned the ranks of the young before they could repay to society the resources and energy devoted to them.[116]

The depopulation of Europe also left many people without spouses. Though most people soon remarried, there were many mismatches in age. Many elderly women, for example, took young men for husbands. Older men also married young girls, often to get possession of the girls' dowries.

As humanity tried to rebound, pregnant females soon became a common sight on the streets of most European communities in the second half of the fourteenth century. But people disagreed about what effect the Black Death had, if any, on fertility. Some chroniclers insisted that the disease made many women barren. Others observed just the opposite. According to Jean de Venette, a Catholic friar in France, "Everywhere women conceived more readily than usual. None proved barren, on the contrary, there were pregnant women wherever you looked. Several gave birth to twins, and some to living triplets."[117]

Despite the spate of new births, the repopulation of Europe was a slow process. Deaths attributed to the plague, along with those from other diseases and war, caused such a tremendous drop in human population in the fourteenth century that Europe needed several centuries to rebuild its population.

The Rise of the Poor

The shortage of manpower changed the economy of Europe. It created an economic boon for the lower classes that few ever anticipated. The vast death toll meant that not enough workers were left to do the daily work needed to make society function efficiently. For the first time in centuries, workers of all kinds were in big demand across Europe. Serfs, freemen, artisans, craftsmen, and church workers no longer felt compelled to live and work under conditions set and enforced by Europe's ruling classes. Now they could work for whomever paid the highest wages. They could also demand better conditions for themselves. Many serfs, for example, requested—and received—oxen and fertilizers to be more productive farmers. Their improved negotiating

With the economic improvements after the plague, serfs were able to work under much better conditions. Some eventually became landowners, plowing and tending to their own crops.

power also meant that some serfs eventually became landowners themselves.

But the rise in the status of serfs also bred arrogance. A chronicler in the cathedral in Rochester, England, observed that, because of the new economic conditions, "the humble turned up their noses at employment, and could scarcely be persuaded to serve the eminent [the upper classes] unless for triple wages."[118]

Though the labor shortage benefited workers, it caused great hardships for others. Food rotted in the fields for lack of workers, and people starved for lack of food. Higher wages for workers also led to inflated prices for goods and services and caused economic uncertainty in the marketplace.

Nobles also resented the rising fortunes of the poor for other reasons. Many were upset that the old social order was changing. Serfs were no longer dependent on their landlords and were less likely to obey them. Many nobles also did not wish to see their own social standing diminished in any way. Such seemed the case when members of the lower classes were able to afford and wear fine clothes that resembled those worn by nobility. In response, many lords and ladies began donning expensive, outlandish clothes to accentuate the differences between themselves and those they considered social inferiors.

Keeping the Poor in Their Place

Swayed by the concerns of the nobility, European rulers issued special "sumptuary laws" to control the economy and to keep peasants in their place. England passed its first Statute of Labourers in 1351 to fix wages of workers at rates that existed before the Black Death. Other laws followed. These rules told employers how much they could pay for labor, and they told workers how much they could charge. They also prescribed what types of clothes the people of the lower classes could wear and forbid them—no matter how much wealth they possessed—from purchasing certain items, including silk or embroidered clothing, that were set aside for the ruling classes only. The new legislation also limited what foods could be served at the weddings of the lower classes and how many mourners could attend a funeral.

One English sumptuary law, decreed in 1363, required,

> that esquires and all gentlemen below the rank of knight, who do not have land or rent worth more than . . . [100 pounds] shall not receive or wear cloth for their garments or stockings worth more than $4\frac{1}{2}$ marks for a whole cloth. . . . Nor wear any cloth of gold, silver or silk; any embroidered garment; any ring, clasp, brooch, ribbon, belt, or any garment or harness [belts, buckles, and straps] of gold or silver; jewels or any kind of fur.[119]

Though the sumptuary laws pleased the nobles, they proved to be unpopular with the poor and were difficult to enforce. English chronicler Henry Knighton observed of his time that workers were "so above themselves and so bloody-minded that they took no notice of the king's command"[120] not to take wages higher than those to which they were accustomed.

In response, the king imposed fines on any employers who paid workers inflated wages. According to Knighton, the monarch also ordered

> numerous workers arrested and sent to prison, and many of these escaped and

took to the woods and if they were captured they were heavily fined. And most took oaths that they would not take more than their old daily wages, and thereby secured their release from prison.[121]

This crackdown only made peasants angrier. Their growing resentment over having their wages set and their opportunities limited may have been at least partly responsible for a series of peasant revolts that shook European life in the late fourteenth century. Many of the alienated poor agreed with Englishman John Ball, who spent twenty years in the mid–fourteenth century sermonizing against social inequality. In one sermon the angry priest declared, "Good people, things will never go well in England so long as goods be not in common, and so long as there be villeins [peasants] and gentlemen. By what right are they whom we call lords greater folk than we?"[122]

Other Long-Lasting Changes

Population shortages caused still other lasting changes to European life. Many landowners, for example, switched from growing grains—an activity that required many workers—to less labor-intensive crops. In England, for instance, many fields were enclosed for the raising of sheep. Farmers in southern Germany planted woad, a European herb whose leaves are used for blue dyestuff.

The need for human labor also sparked human inventiveness. Increasingly, Europeans sought technological solutions to problems caused by the lack of workers. For example, new water mills and windmills appeared in parts of Europe to make up for the shortfall of human labor. Another big change came in the production of books. A shortage of scribes— men who copied books by hand—helped to

A shortage of scribes helped spark the invention of the first printing press in 1450.

stimulate the invention of the movable-type printing press sometime around 1450.

Because physicians were in short supply for many decades after the Black Death subsided, medical colleges had faculty openings for years. But as these positions were eventually filled, medical science took off in a new direction. New personnel brought new ideas. In addition, the failure of the medical establishment during the plague sparked a continuing quest for accurate and useful information. No longer were physicians content with the old medical knowledge. Increasingly, teaching in medical schools reflected the importance of anatomy and the scientific method rather than the ideas of the ancient Greeks.

Hospitals saw improvements, too. Before the Black Death, many of these institutions were little more than homes for the poor that took in the elderly, widows, and orphans. During epidemics, they sheltered the sick mostly to isolate them from the healthy, not to cure them. But after the Black Death, more hospitals became health centers in which doctors also tried to heal their patients.

The Black Death also left the general public more curious about health and disease than ever before. Cities throughout Europe created new health and sanitary codes. New boards of health were established in Florence, Venice, Nuremberg, Milan, and other cities. Their responsibilities included reporting all epidemics, isolating the sick, and controlling the movement of people in and out of the infected areas.

The cumulative impact of all of the changes wrought by the Black Death was powerful and long lasting. Added together, they contributed to an even greater transformation in Europe: the eventual collapse of the feudal system, a way of life that had lasted for centuries.

The End of the Dark Ages

Before the plague's arrival, Europe's three-layered medieval social structure—the Catholic Church, the nobility, and the peasantry—was already declining. A rising class of merchants, along with new cities and improvements in agriculture, weakened the foundations of the medieval world. Then the Black Death appeared and delivered a powerful blow to medieval society, sending it staggering into oblivion.

The fading of the Middle Ages was a mixed blessing for many Europeans. As the old society changed into something new, many people discovered that their lives changed for better and for worse. Most poor people were freed of many of the feudal bonds that once held them in near slavery. But this newfound freedom came with costs.

English Sumptuary Laws

The scarcity of working people caused by the Black Death contributed to severe economic problems. In response, English lawmakers implemented new laws like the following, which was passed on June 18, 1349. The extract comes from Rosemary Horrox's *The Black Death*.

"Since a great part of the population, and especially workers and employees, has now died in this pestilence many people, observing the needs of masters and the shortage of employees, are refusing to work unless they are paid an excessive salary. Others prefer to beg in idleness rather than work for their living. Mindful of the serious inconvenience likely to arise from this shortage, especially of agricultural labourers, we have discussed and considered the matter with our prelates and nobles and other learned men and, with their unanimous advice, we have ordained that every man or woman in our realm of England, whether free or unfree, who is physically fit and below the age of sixty, not living by trade or by exercising a particular craft and not having private means or land of their own upon which they need to work, and not working for someone else, shall, if offered employment consonant with their status, be obliged to accept the employment offered. . . .

And if any man or woman . . . refuses . . . then let the person be immediately arrested . . . and set to the nearest gaol [jail] . . . until they will accept employment."

After the Black Death, a rising class of merchants helped weaken the stronghold of feudalism in Europe.

Gone were the days of protection, self-sufficiency, and a shared sense of community that Europeans enjoyed on feudal manors for centuries. Shorn of the overriding power of religious authority, Europeans also felt more disposed than ever before to focus on the physical and material, rather than spiritual, aspects of life. Altogether, writes historian Robert S. Gottfried, these changes in everyday life meant a new "growing emphasis on individualism, one of the important characteristics that scholars regard as typically modern." [123]

Finally, the Black Death also forced on all Europeans who survived its deadly rampage a deep sense of respect and fear of the power of nature. Like millions of other survivors of the plague, the poet Petrarch possessed this dark knowledge. And he wondered if anyone in the future could possibly ever believe what happened in his day:

> Will posterity ever believe these things when we, who see, can scarcely credit them? We should think we were dreaming if we did not with our eyes, when we walk abroad, see the city in mourning with funerals, and returning to our home, find it empty, and thus know that what we lament is real. [124]

Today, only the words of the dead, now frozen on manuscripts, can testify to the living that the terror of the Black Death was no dream.

Notes

Introduction: Century of Death

1. Frederick F. Cartwright, in collaboration with Michael D. Biddis, *Disease and History.* New York: Dorset, 1972, p. 38.
2. Charles L. Mee Jr., "How a Mysterious Disease Laid Low Europe's Masses," *Smithsonian*, February 1990, p. 69.
3. H. G. Wells, *The Outline of History: Being the Plain History of Life and Mankind*, rev. ed. Garden City, NY: Garden City Books, 1961, p. 592.
4. Quoted in Robert S. Gottfried, *The Black Death: Natural and Human Disaster in Medieval Europe.* New York: Free, 1983, p. 16.

Chapter 1: Life in Fourteenth-Century Europe

5. Will Durant, *The Age of Faith.* New York: Simon and Schuster, 1950, pp. 561–62.
6. Quoted in *Readings in World History.* Orlando, FL: Harcourt, Brace, Jovanovich; Holt, Rinehart, and Winston, 1990, pp. 73–74.
7. Gottfried, *The Black Death*, p. 162.
8. E. R. Chamberlin, *Everyday Life in Renaissance Times.* New York: G. P. Putnam's Sons, 1965, p. 114.
9. Quoted in Gottfried, *The Black Death*, p. 28.

Chapter 2: The Spread of the Black Death

10. Quoted in Mee, "How a Mysterious Disease Laid Low Europe's Masses," p. 69.
11. Quoted in Francis Aidan Gasquet, *The Black Death of 1348 and 1349.* London: George Bell and Sons, 1908, p. 6.
12. Quoted in Gasquet, *The Black Death of 1348 and 1349*, p. 7.
13. Quoted in Rosemary Horrox, trans. and ed., *The Black Death.* Manchester, England: Manchester University Press, 1994, p. 19.
14. Quoted in Gasquet, *The Black Death of 1348 and 1349*, p. 162.
15. Quoted in Gottfried, *The Black Death*, p. 42.
16. Quoted in Gottfried, *The Black Death*, p. 41.
17. Gasquet, *The Black Death of 1348 and 1349*, pp. 12–13.
18. Quoted in Johannes Nohl, *The Black Death: A Chronicle of the Plague Compiled from Contemporary Sources*, trans. C. H. Clarke. London: Unwin Books, 1961, p. 10.
19. Giovanni Boccaccio, *The Decameron.* New York: Garden City, 1949, p. 2.
20. Boccaccio, *The Decameron*, p. 6.
21. Boccaccio, *The Decameron*, p. 6.
22. Gottfried, *The Black Death*, p. 49.
23. Quoted in Gasquet, *The Black Death of 1348 and 1349*, p. 42.
24. Quoted in Gasquet, *The Black Death of 1348 and 1349*, p. 46.
25. Quoted in Sir Arthur Bryant, *The Age of Chivalry: The Atlantic Saga* Garden City, NY: Doubleday, 1963, pp. 381–82.
26. Quoted in Gasquet, *The Black Death of 1348 and 1349*, p. 51.

27. Quoted in Horrox, *The Black Death*, p. 53.

28. Quoted in Gasquet, *The Black Death of 1348 and 1349*, p. 52.

29. Quoted in Gasquet, *The Black Death of 1348 and 1349*, p. 55.

30. Quoted in Gasquet, *The Black Death of 1348 and 1349*, p. 76.

31. Quoted in Gasquet, *The Black Death of 1348 and 1349*, p. 70.

32. Quoted in Bryant, *The Age of Chivalry*, p. 382.

33. Bryant, *The Age of Chivalry*, p. 383.

34. Quoted in Horrox, *The Black Death*, p. 74.

35. Quoted in Bryant, *The Age of Chivalry*, p. 379.

36. Quoted in Bryant, *The Age of Chivalry*, p. 379.

37. Quoted in Horrox, *The Black Death*, p. 64.

38. Quoted in Bryant, *The Age of Chivalry*, p. 383.

39. Quoted in Bryant, *The Age of Chivalry*, p. 384.

40. Quoted in Bryant, *The Age of Chivalry*, p. 384.

41. Quoted in Horrox, *The Black Death*, p. 69.

42. Quoted in Horrox, *The Black Death*, p. 78.

43. Quoted in Horrox, *The Black Death*, p. 84.

44. Quoted in Gasquet, *The Black Death of 1348 and 1349*, p. 79.

45. Gasquet, *The Black Death of 1348 and 1349*, p. 73.

Chapter 3: Dealing with the Dead and Dying

46. Boccaccio, *The Decameron*, p. 3.

47. Quoted in Philip Ziegler, *The Black Death*. New York: Harper and Row, 1969, p. 58.

48. Quoted in Horrox, *The Black Death*, p. 60.

49. Quoted in Barbara W. Tuchman, *A Distant Mirror: The Calamitous Fourteenth-Century*. New York: Alfred A. Knopf, 1984, p. 98.

50. Quoted in David Herlitly, *The Black Death and the Transformation of the West*. Cambridge, MA: Harvard University Press, 1997, p. 56.

51. Quoted in Ziegler, *The Black Death*, p. 132.

52. Quoted in Horrox, *The Black Death*, p. 195.

53. Quoted in Horrox, *The Black Death*, p. 203.

54. Quoted in Ziegler, *The Black Death*, p. 156.

55. Quoted in Horrox, *The Black Death*, pp. 51–52.

56. Boccaccio, *The Decameron*, p. 6.

57. Boccaccio, *The Decameron*, p. 5.

58. Quoted in Nohl, *The Black Death*, p. 23.

59. Boccaccio, *The Decameron*, p. 6.

60. Quoted in Gasquet, *The Black Death of 1348 and 1349*, p. 21.

61. Quoted in *Readings in World History*, p. 83.

62. Gasquet, *The Black Death of 1348 and 1349*, p. 23.

63. Quoted in Bryant, *The Age of Chivalry*, p. 385.

64. Quoted in William M. Bowsky, ed., *The Black Death: A Turning Point in History?* New York: Holt, Rinehart, and Winston, 1971, p. 13.

65. Quoted in Nohl, *The Black Death*, p. 101.

66. Nohl, *The Black Death*, p. 101.
67. Boccaccio, *The Decameron*, p. 3.
68. Boccaccio, *The Decameron*, p. 3.
69. Nohl, *The Black Death*, p. 127.
70. Quoted in Horrox, *The Black Death*, p. 61.

Chapter 4: Looking for Answers

71. Quoted in Geoffrey Marks and William K. Beatty, *Epidemics*. New York: Charles Scribner's Sons, 1976, pp. 86–87.
72. Quoted in Bowsky, *The Black Death*, p. 14.
73. Nohl, *The Black Death*, p. 78.
74. Quoted in Horrox, *The Black Death*, p. 23.
75. Quoted in Nohl, *The Black Death*, p. 35.
76. Quoted in Horrox, *The Black Death*, p. 45.
77. Quoted in Abba Eban, *Heritage: Civilization and the Jews.* New York: Summit Books, 1984, p. 169.
78. Gottfried, *The Black Death*, p. 111.
79. Quoted in Gottfried, *The Black Death*, p. 111.
80. Quoted in Horrox, *The Black Death*, p. 59.
81. Quoted in Joseph R. Strayer, ed., *Dictionary of the Middle Ages*, vol. 2. New York: Charles Scribner's Sons, 1983, p. 264.
82. Quoted in Nohl, *The Black Death*, p. 33.
83. Nohl, *The Black Death*, p. 1.
84. Quoted in Horrox, *The Black Death*, p. 154.
85. Quoted in Ziegler, *The Black Death*, p. 112.
86. Quoted in Horrox, *The Black Death*, p. 131.

87. Quoted in Nohl, *The Black Death*, p. 114.
88. Eban, *Heritage*, p. 170.
89. Quoted in Horrox, *The Black Death*, p. 45.
90. Quoted in Nohl, *The Black Death*, p. 124.
91. Quoted in Horrox, *The Black Death*, p. 222.

Chapter 5: Help, Hope, and Healing

92. Jonathan Miller, *The Body in Question*. New York: Vintage Books, 1978, p. 225.
93. Quoted in Horrox, *The Black Death*, p. 124.
94. Nohl, *The Black Death*, p. 65.
95. Quoted in Nohl, *The Black Death*, p. 60.
96. Quoted in Horrox, *The Black Death*, p. 186.
97. Quoted in Nohl, *The Black Death*, p. 61.
98. Ziegler, *The Black Death*, p. 74.
99. Quoted in Nohl, *The Black Death*, p. 58.
100. Quoted in Strayer, *Dictionary of the Middle Ages*, p. 257.
101. Boccaccio, *The Decameron*, p. 2.
102. Nohl, *The Black Death*, p. 83.
103. Quoted in Ziegler, *The Black Death*, p. 91.
104. Quoted in Horrox, *The Black Death*, p. 150.
105. Quoted in Nohl, *The Black Death*, p. 135.

Chapter 6: An Altered Way of Life

106. Mee, "How a Mysterious Disease Laid Low Europe's Masses," p. 76.
107. Gottfried, *The Black Death*, p. 103.
108. Quoted in Bryant, *The Age of Chivalry*, pp. 389–90.

109. Quoted in Horrox, *The Black Death*, p. 75.

110. Gottfried, *The Black Death*, p. 90.

111. Quoted in Horrox, *The Black Death*, p. 347.

112. Quoted in Horrox, *The Black Death*, p. 347.

113. Nohl, *The Black Death*, p. 155.

114. Quoted in Herlitly, *The Black Death and the Transformation of the West*, p. 67.

115. Tuchman, *A Distant Mirror*, p. 117.

116. Herlitly, *The Black Death and the Transformation of the West*, p. 44.

117. Quoted in Horrox, *The Black Death*, p. 57.

118. Quoted in Horrox, *The Black Death*, p. 70.

119. Quoted in Horrox, *The Black Death*, p. 341.

120. Quoted in Horrox, *The Black Death*, p. 79.

121. Quoted in Horrox, *The Black Death*, p. 79.

122. Quoted in Wells, *The Outline of History*, p. 593.

123. Gottfried, *The Black Death*, p. 162.

124. Quoted in Gasquet, *The Black Death of 1348 and 1349*, pp. 33–34.

Chronology of Events

541–542
Plague of Justinian becomes first recorded pandemic form of the Black Death.

950–1250
European population triples from 25 million to 75 million; revival of towns and cities begins.

1315–1317
Famine strikes Europe.

1320–1322
The Black Death first appears in Mongolia.

1320–1347
The Black Death kills 25 million in China, India, and other areas of Asia; outbreaks appear in the Mideast, Persia, Asia Minor, Greece, and Africa; the plague spreads westward along trade routes.

1346
Hostilities erupt between Tatars and Genoan traders in Kaffa; Italian ships bring Black Death to Genoa, Italy.

1347
Black Death arrives in Messina, Sicily; spreads to all of Sicily and Venice.

1348–1349
The plague rages through most of Italy and spreads into France, the Low Countries, Spain, Switzerland, Austria, Germany, Poland, Hungary, the Balkans, the British Isles, Scandinavia, Iceland, and Greenland; attacks on Jewish populations in France, Germany, Austria, Spain, Italy, and parts of Central Europe; flagellant movement is underway in Germany, France, the Low Countries, and eastern Europe.

1349
Pope Clement II orders flagellants to disband; within a year, the movement is gone.

1351
The first sumptuary laws are passed to regulate wages in England; the Black Death spreads into Russia; staff for the pope report that the Black Death killed 24 million.

1352
The Black Death has run its course in most European nations.

1361
The plague returns as an epidemic.

1363
The plague returns as an epidemic.

1369
The plague returns as an epidemic.

1371
The plague returns as an epidemic.

1390
The plague returns as an epidemic.

1394
The pope bans social gatherings in graveyards.

1405
The plague returns as an epidemic.

1665–1666
The Great Plague of London occurs.

For Further Reading

Morris Bishop and the editors of Horizon Magazine, *The Horizon Book of the Middle Ages*. New York: American Heritage, 1968. A history of the medieval period for the general reader.

Mike Corbishley et al., *The Young Oxford History of Britain and Ireland*. Oxford, England: Oxford University Press, 1996. A readable and richly illustrated volume for young adults.

Phyllis Corzine, *The Black Death*. San Diego: Lucent Books, 1997. A readable chronological treatment of the plague filled with primary sources and illustrations.

Michael Worth Davison, ed., *Everyday Life Through the Dark Ages*. London: Reader's Digest, 1992. A well-illustrated and readable history of the Middle Ages.

Editors of Time-Life Books, *The Age of Calamity: Time Frame AD 1300-1400*. Alexandria, VA: Time-Life Books, 1991. A very readable and concise history of the fourteenth century that includes interesting passages on the Black Death.

Works Consulted

Nathan Ausubel, *Pictorial History of the Jewish People: From Bible Times to Our Own Day Throughout the World.* New York: Crown, 1984. An interesting and well-researched history of the Jewish people for the general reader.

Arthur E. R. Boak et al., *The History of Our World.* Boston: Houghton Mifflin, 1961. A high-school textbook.

Giovanni Boccaccio, *The Decameron.* New York; Garden City, 1949. This literary masterpiece of world history provides the most vivid and commonly quoted accounts of the Black Death.

William M. Bowsky, ed., *The Black Death: A Turning Point in History?* New York: Holt, Rinehart, and Winston, 1971. A collection of passages written by those who experienced the Black Death first hand and scholarly articles about the disease.

Derek Brewer, *Chaucer and His World.* New York: Dodd, Mead, 1978. A handsomely illustrated and informative book about the life of the famous English poet and the world in which he lived.

Sir Arthur Bryant, *The Age of Chivalry: The Atlantic Saga.* Garden City, NY: Doubleday, 1963. A readable, scholarly work on life in the Middle Ages.

Frederick F. Cartwright, in collaboration with Michael D. Biddis, *Disease and History.* New York: Dorset, 1972. A scholarly yet lively look at the impact of several major diseases on the course of world history.

E. R. Chamberlin, *Everyday Life in Renaissance Times.* New York: G. P. Putnam's Sons, 1965. This book lives up to its title in a very readable and informative manner.

Will Durant, *The Age of Faith.* New York: Simon and Schuster, 1950. A readable and very scholarly work on the history of medieval civilization by one of the best-known popularizers of history.

Abba Eban, *Heritage: Civilization and the Jews.* New York: Summit Books, 1984. A readable illustrated history of the Jewish people by a renowned Israeli author, statesman, and diplomat.

Francis Aidan Gasquet, *The Black Death of 1348 and 1349.* London: George Bell and Sons, 1908. A scholarly and readable work for researchers and lay readers alike.

Frances and Joseph Gies, *Life in a Medieval Village.* New York: Harper & Row, 1990. An informative and in-depth look at the daily life of medieval villagers.

Robert S. Gottfried, *The Black Death: Natural and Human Disaster in Medieval Europe.* New York: Free, 1983. A scholarly yet readable account of the Black Death.

John R. Green, *Medical History for Students.* Springfield, IL: Charles C. Thomas, 1968. A dated yet informative text for general readers.

Gertrude Hartman, *Medieval Days and Ways.* New York: Macmillan, 1965. A readable general survey of different facets of everyday life during the Middle Ages.

David Herlitly, *The Black Death and the Transformation of the West.* Cambridge, MA: Harvard University Press, 1997. A concise, scholarly analysis of the historical impact of the plague.

Rosemary Horrox, trans. and ed., *The Black Death*. Manchester, England: Manchester University Press, 1994. An invaluable collection of primary sources covering a wide variety of topics associated with the Black Death.

Arno Karlen, *Man and Microbes: Disease and Plagues in History and Modern Times*. New York: G. P. Putnam's Sons, 1995. A book for general audiences that looks at the impact of various diseases on humanity.

George C. Kohn, ed., *Encyclopedia of Plague and Pestilence*. New York: Facts On File, 1995. An encyclopedia of historical, medical, and cultural facts concerning various deadly diseases in history.

Maynard Mack, ed., *The Continental Edition of World Masterpieces*. Vol. 1. New York: W. W. Norton, 1966. A compilation of literary works from around the world, ranging from biblical times to the mid-1600s.

Geoffrey Marks and William K. Beatty, *Epidemics*. New York: Charles Scribner's Sons, 1976. A fascinating book filled with quotes from primary sources about the great epidemics of history.

Charles L. Mee Jr., "How a Mysterious Disease Laid Low Europe's Masses," *Smithsonian*, February 1990. A lengthy article that summarizes the Black Death's history.

Dorothy Miller, *The Middle Ages*. New York: G. P. Putnam's Sons, 1935. A readable history of the Middle Ages for the general reader.

Jonathan Miller, *The Body in Question*. New York: Vintage Books, 1978. An interesting history of the discovery of the workings of the human body written by a popular British writer, actor, and physician.

Bishop Morris, *The Middle Ages*. New York: American Heritage, 1970. A highly readable survey of the medieval period by a renowned scholar.

Johannes Nohl, *The Black Death: A Chronicle of the Plague Compiled from Contemporary Sources*. Trans. C. H. Clarke. London: Unwin Books, 1961. This reprint of the 1926 original is a fascinating narrative based on primary sources that reveal a vast array of human responses to the Black Death.

Readings in World History. Orlando, FL: Harcourt, Brace, Jovanovich; Holt, Rinehart, and Winston, 1990. A collection of primary sources from firsthand observers of major events in world history.

Joseph R. Strayer, ed., *Dictionary of the Middle Ages*. Vol. 2. New York: Charles Scribner's Sons, 1983. A multivolume encyclopedic survey of the Middle Ages.

Barbara W. Tuchman, *A Distant Mirror: The Calamitous Fourteenth-Century*. New York: Alfred A. Knopf, 1984. An intimate, detailed look at one of the most calamitous centuries in history.

H. G. Wells, *The Outline of History: Being the Plain History of Life and Mankind*. Rev. ed. Garden City, NY: Garden City Books, 1961. A readable history for the general reader by a popular writer.

Philip Ziegler, *The Black Death*. New York: Harper and Row, 1969. An often cited source, this volume is well written and comprehensive.

Index

Clement VI (pope)
   on death toll, 31
   on defense of Jews, 56
   preventive measures of, 61
climate
   famine and, 23
   as punishment of God,
      33–34
   spread of Black Death and,
      9
   as suspected cause of Black
      Death, 51
clothing, 15, 78
Clynn, John, 35–37
Colle, Dionysius, 61
Compagnia della Misericordia, 45
crime
   breakdown of society and,
      46
   punishments for, 21
cross brethren (cross brothers), 66–69
Crusades, 18

"Dance of Death," 74
Death, the. See Black Death
death toll
   in Asia, 24
   of doctors, 64
   in England, 34, 35
   in Europe, 8, 11, 76–77
   in France, 31–32, 44
   in Islamic world, 27
   in Italy, 28–29, 30, 40
   in Scotland, 35
   in Spain, 32
Decameron, The (Boccaccio),
   22, 29
de Chauliac, Guy, 32
   on behavior of doctors, 64
   on plagues in Avignon, 44
   on training and duties of
      surgeons, 67

de Covino, Simon, 31
de Mussis, Gabriele
   on Black Death as punish-
      ment of God, 49–50
   on Black Death in Messina,
      27
   on burials, 44
   on misery caused by Black
      Death, 30
   on spread of Black Death,
      25, 26
Dene, William, 71
Denmark, 37
de Venette, Jean
   on births after Black
      Death, 77
   on death toll in Paris, 44
   on omens of Black Death,
      46
diet, 14–15, 62–63
Disease and History
   (Cartwright and Biddis), 8
diseases, 23
di Tura, Agnolo
   on abandonment of sick, 38
   on psychological effects of
      Black Death, 49
Durant, Will, 15

earthquakes, 51
Eban, Abba, 55, 56
England
   death toll in, 34
   Jews in, 56
   London
      burials in, 44
      death toll in, 35
      government of, 40
   peasant revolt, 15
   serfs in, 13
   spread of of Black Death
      in, 34–35
   sumptuary laws, 78, 80
   weather in, 33–34

enteric plague, 11
environment, 24

farming
   effect of Black Death on,
      30, 78, 79
   inventions and, 18
   weather and, 23, 70
flagellants, 66–69, 72
fleas, 8–9
food, 14–15, 62–63
France
   crime in, 46
   death toll in, 31–32
   Marseilles, 31–32
   Paris
      death toll in, 44
      population of, 20
   serfs in, 13
   spread of Black Death in,
      31–32
funerals, 41–42, 43–45, 74

Galen, 58
Garbo, 63
Gasquet, Francis Aidan
   on funerals, 44
   on spread of Black Death,
      37
   on symptoms of Black
      Death, 27–28
Germany, 32, 75
Gies, Frances
   on meals of nobles, 15
   on peasant revolt, 15
Gies, Joseph
   on meals of nobles, 15
   on peasant revolt, 15
God's tokens, 35
Gottfried, Robert S.
   on death toll in Italy, 30
   on funerals, 74
   on growth of individualism,
      81

on importance of religion, 17
on psychological effects of Black Death, 72
on suspected causes of Black Death, 51
Great Mortality. *See* Black Death
Great Pestilence. *See* Black Death
Great Plague. *See* Black Death
Grim Reaper, 74
Gypsies, 56

Hecker, J. F., 49
Heinrich of Herford, 69
Herlity, David, 76–77
Heyligen, Louis, 55
Hippocrates, 50
homes
  of merchants, 20–21
  of nobles, 14–15
  of peasants, 13–14
Hungary, 32
Huss, John, 71

Ibn Khaldun, 27
inventions, 18, 79
Ireland, 35–36
Italy
  crime in, 46
  death toll in, 28–29, 30
  Florence
    burials in, 45
    death toll in, 29
    population of, 20
  Genoa
    population of, 20
    spread of Black Death to, 26
  Messina, 26–27
  Milan, 40
    quarantines in, 40

Siena, 44–45
spread of Black Death in, 26–29
Venice
  burials in, 44
  population of, 20
  spread of Black Death to, 26
"It Is Good to Think on Death," 74–75

Jews, 51, 54–56, 69
John of Burgundy, 62
John of Fordum, 38
John of Reading
  on effect of Black Death on morality, 73
  on weather in England prior to Black Death, 33

Kaffa, 24–26
Knighton, Henry
  on appearance of Black Death in Scotland, 35
  on sumptuary laws, 78–79
  on weather in England prior to Black Death, 33–34
knights, 12, 20

languages, 72
lepers, 56
Life in a Medieval Village (Gies and Gies), 15
Li Muisis, Gilles, 32
literacy, 16
Lithuania, 56
Low Countries, 32
Luciferians, 72

Magnus II (king of Sweden), 53
Marsilio, 63
medicine, 17

after Black Death, 79–80
beak doctors, 61, 62
Catholic Church and, 57–58
doctors
  behavior of, 64
  death toll of, 64
  training and duties of, 67
preventive measures, 8, 60–64
treatments, 8, 58–60
Mee, Charles L., Jr.
  on ability of rat flea to find a host, 9
  on origins of "Ring Around the Rosy," 48
  on psychological effects of Black Death, 70–71
merchants, 19–20
Michael of Piazza, 26–27
Middle Ages, 12, 18, 80–81
middle class, 19–20
Miller, Jonathan, 58
Monatti, 46
moneylending, 54, 56
morality plays, 21
Mortus, 46
Muslims, 56
mystery plays, 21

nobles, 12, 13
  after Black Death, 78
  life of, 14–16
  merchants and, 19–20
  serfs and, 20
Nohl, Johannes
  on Angel of Death, 53
  on behavior of uninfected, 48
  on Black Death as Apocalypse, 49
  on crime, 46
  on fixation on death, 75
  on Plague Maiden, 53

on preventive measures, 61
on use of relics, 65
Norway, 37

omens, 46

Paré, Ambroise, 46
peasants
life of, 12–14
revolts of, 15, 79
see also serfs
Petrarch
on Black Death, 81
poem to Laura, 73
pilgrimages, 65, 71
Plague Maiden, 53
Plague of Florence. *See* Black
Death
plagues
carriers, 8–9
environment and, 24
recurrence of, 11, 70
symptoms of, 9–11, 22,
27–28, 44
types, 9–11
see also Black Death
pneumonic plague, 10–11
Poland, 32, 56
population
Black Death and. *See* death
toll
famine and, 23
growth of, 18, 23, 77
preventive measures, 8
medical, 40, 60–64
religious, 33, 65–69
Protestant Reformation, 71
Prussia, 32

quarantines, 40

rats, 8–9, 14, 23

reading, 16
relics, 19, 65
religion
Black Death as punish-
ment, 35, 49–50, 53–54
mystery and morality plays,
21
prevention of Black Death
and, 33, 60, 64, 65–69
see also Catholic Church
Rhasis, 64
Righi, Alessandro, 38–39
"Ring Around the Rosy," 48
Roman Empire, 12
Russia, 46

St. Sebastian, 65
sanitation
after Black Death, 80
burials and, 22
in cities, 22–23
Jews and, 54
as preventive measure, 62
spread of Black Death and,
40, 51
Satan, 53
Scandinavia, 37
science, 17
Scotland, 35
septicemic plague, 11
Sercambi, 28–29
serfs
after Black Death, 77–78
independence of, 18
life of, 12–14
nobles and, 20
revolts of, 15, 79
Spain, 32
Statute of Labourers, 78
sumptuary laws, 78–79, 80
supernatural, 53
superstitions, 13, 17, 46

swarta doden. *See* Black
Death
Sweden, 37

Tatars, 25
"Three Adverb Pills," 64
towns. *See* cities
trade
growth of cities and, 18–19
spread of Black Death and,
24, 31, 37
treatments, 8, 58–60
Tuchman, Barbara W., 76
Twinger, Jacob, 56

Villani, Giovanni, 23, 29
violence, 73–74
Visconti, Bernabo, 40

weather
famine and, 23
as punishment of God,
33–34
spread of Black Death and,
9
as suspected cause of Black
Death, 51
Wells, H. G., 11
William of Nangis, 32
witches, 56
wolves, 43
Wycliffe, John, 71

Xenopsylla cheopis (rat flea),
8–9

Yersina pestis (bacterium),
8–9

Ziegler, Philip, 64

Picture Credits

About the Author

John M. Dunn is a freelance writer and high-school history teacher. He has taught in Georgia, Florida, North Carolina, and Germany. As a writer and journalist, he has published over 275 articles and stories in more than 20 periodicals as well as scripts for audiovisual productions and a children's play. His books *The Russian Revolution*, *The Relocation of the North American Indian*, *The Spread of Islam*, *Advertising*, *The Civil Rights Movement*, and *The Enlightenment* are published by Lucent Books. He lives with his wife and two daughters in Ocala, Florida.